SILVER DONALD CAMERON

SEASONS IN THE RAIN

An Expatriate's Notes on British Columbia

McClelland and Stewart

McClelland and Stewart Limited,
The Canadian Publishers,
25 Hollinger Road,
Toronto, Ontario.
M4B 3G2

Printed and bound in Canada

Canadian Cataloguing in Publication Data

Cameron, Donald, 1937-
  Seasons in the rain

ISBN 0-7710-1847-9 pa.

1. British Columbia - Biography. I. Title.

FC3805.C34   971.1'00992   C77-001695-2
F1086.8.C34

CONTENTS

To the gingery little lady
on West 23rd Avenue,
an ardent Vancouverite
from Treherne, Manitoba,
my mother

INTRODUCTION: The Mountains of Gold

Gold in the mountains. Timber in the mountains. Grass beyond the mountains. Lead and zinc, coal and pelts in the mountains. A rich and difficult country.

The Chinese character which now signifies "North America" originally meant "the mountains of gold," and indeed, an actual gold rush prompted the British to establish British Columbia as an organized Crown Colony in 1858. Observe two points which mark the province's history from the beginning: people went there to get rich, and most of the people in the province are comparatively recent arrivals.

Only a bit over a century ago, in 1862, a young Englishman went looking for coal at what is still called Coal Harbour in

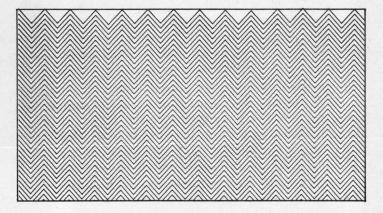

downtown Vancouver, and felt it prudent to keep clear of the present site of Lumbermen's Arch, where 2,000 Salish warriors were preparing for a raid by Haida slavers. Thirty years later, the city was being eulogized by Rudyard Kipling. By 1937 Stephen Leacock could rhapsodize over a city with "the combined excellence of nature's gift and man's handiwork" and compare its shopping district to those of London and Paris. And yet when Leacock wrote, there were men alive who could remember the days before even a trail had been cut through the enormous firs that covered the site of the city's centre.

So much has been achieved in so short a time, both in Vancouver and in the province at large, that British Columbians tend to assume that anything is possible, and they remain marvellously willing to experiment with everything from government and drugs to food and domestic architecture. West Coast writers are the most innovative in the country, and the province has an international reputation as a centre for the relatively novel process of ferro-cement boatbuilding. B.C. communities, in general, are eager to accept and enfold newcomers and to treat them as permanent citizens almost before their suitcases are unpacked, particularly if they are white, English-speaking, and infatuated with their new home.

But the province's youthfulness is also rootlessness: hence its comical impulse to purchase an instant history and ancestry. Gold rush towns are lovingly restored, scholarly histories are commissioned,* and B.C. is surely the only jurisdiction on earth to celebrate three centennials in thirteen years: in 1958, for the centennial of its founding; in 1967, for the centennial of the country it now adorns; and again in 1971, for the centennial of its turbulent entry into Confederation.

My own roots in B.C. are, by comparison, relatively deep, for "Pap" Cameron, my father's father, is buried in a cleft in the mountains of the West Kootenays, in Nelson, the nearest thing to an ancestral village that my nomadic family can claim. My father finished school in Nelson; his surviving brother and sister both live in the immediate area, and whenever I cross the Koote-

*Margaret Ormsby, *British Columbia: A History* (1958). By contrast, Nova Scotia's longer, richer history is still not captured in a good one-volume work.

nay River and start up the long hill at Taghum, it feels as though part of me is coming home.

After college, my father became principal of the high school in the papermilling town of Powell River–the newer high school in nearby Westview is named after him–and there he met and courted the home economics teacher. They were married in her native Manitoba, in 1933, and immediately moved east, where he won his Ph.D. and taught at the University of Toronto. I was thus accidentally born in Ontario, four years later. Nobody asked me: I would have preferred to wait and do it in B.C. By the time my brothers were born, the family was securely settled in Vancouver, in the house my mother still lives in. When we came to the Coast, I was two. I would be over thirty before I saw Toronto again. As far as I could see, it hadn't changed much.

I came to Vancouver in 1939. I left for good in 1964, when I was twenty-seven. In between, I had lived and studied and worked mostly in Vancouver, but also in the Fraser Valley, up the coast at Gibson's Landing and Powell River, in the West Kootenays and the Kettle Valley, and, for a year, in California. In August, 1964, my wife and I and our first two children left by train from the old CPR station at the foot of Granville Street. On the face of it, we were only going for two or three years of graduate study in England, but we knew we were not coming back.

My first visit back came in 1971, after seven years of Europe and the Maritimes, after a Ph.D. and college teaching, after two more children and a separation, after a plunge into journalism. I was working on two books–*Conversations with Canadian Novelists* and *The Education of Everett Richardson*–and I had a commission from *Saturday Night* to do a profile of Homer Stevens. I discovered that I had an interesting view of the West Coast. I knew it deeply, but by now I saw it also from an outsider's perspective; it was part of me, but I was no longer part of it; in my thirties I was viewing the scenes of my youth, but many of them had changed. The experience was powerful, peculiar, provocative.

Since then I have been back half a dozen times, for periods ranging from six hours to six weeks. Usually I have contrived to have some institution pay the bloated cost of crossing this country–*Weekend* Magazine, the Canada Council, the Writers'

9

Union. My mother likes to point out that a federal government concerned with national unity in *all* its aspects would by now have devised a fare structure to encourage Canadians to know their own country; our absurd fares make it far more practical for a Maritimer to travel to Europe or the Caribbean than to B.C. She has expressed this opinion to the boys in Ottawa, who have paid very little more attention to her than they do to the rest of us. They'll be sorry.

The essays in this book are a result of those subsidized, sentimental journeys. Most of them were published in a slightly different form in *Weekend*, to which I was a contributing editor for a couple of years, and I am deeply grateful to the magazine and especially to its former editor, Sheena Paterson, without whose support and encouragement many of them would never have been written. A good editor makes a writer feel that his or her work is a delight, a constant revelation, and an important statement; such an editor demands–and provokes–a writer's best efforts. For me, Sheena was an editor of that rare kind, and the years working with her and with the sparkling group of people she gathered around her–particularly Jacqui Bishop and Bob Stall–were among the most productive and pleasant periods of my working life. Even the title of this book was the inspiration of someone at *Weekend*. I never knew who thought of it, but I'm grateful.

Despite its subtitle, this is not really a book about the province itself. It is a book about some of the people who have come to British Columbia, and very few of them actually began their lives in the Pacific province; they come from China, from Austria, from Holland, from eastern Canada. Five of them were originally English. Somewhere I have read that of the people who live in B.C., only about 40 per cent were actually born there. In the Maritimes, by contrast, the figure is over 97 per cent.

These, then, are some of the British Columbians who interest me, and around them cohere various themes I think are revealing about the whole community. Here is the right-wing charmer, David Hancock; the civil libertarian, Donald Brown; and the Communist, Homer Stevens; taken together, a fair representation of the schizoid variety of B.C. politics. My own politics, of course, are also pretty obvious: I notice that I have chosen to write about artists, scholars and working people, about anarchists and union officers, about world sailors and about the Doukhobors.

Nothing much about elected "leaders" and the Beautiful People. No story on Art Phillips and Carole Taylor, nothing about the stuffy pragmatism of Bill Bennett or the chunky charm of Dave Barrett. Not a word about the MacMillans, the Clynes, the Woodwards, the Farrises, the Bell-Irvings. No recital of economic statistics, no great paintings of landscapes, no travelogues to speak of. Just a couple of dozen people living out their lives by the ocean or in the mountains. But I think they tell a larger story.

I have made very few changes in the text, aside from offering full-length versions of essays which in several cases were heavily cut for magazine publication. Some anomalies result from this: in these pages, Jack Wasserman lives on, Dave Barrett rules Victoria, Homer Stevens is still president of the United Fishermen and Allied Workers' Union. Troublesome, but one hardly knows what to do about it. The *mood* of 1977 is different from that of, say, 1972 or 1974; if I were to rewrite the Homer Stevens profile, I would have to update not only the facts, but also the assumptions and perhaps the style. Better to leave the articles with their dates, as observations from a particular station in time.

I said earlier that I knew in 1964 that I would not be coming back to B.C. to live. In part, that choice was made for specific professional reasons. I was going to be a university teacher, and at that time there was really only one university in the province, the University of British Columbia. The University of Victoria was still just a junior college with ideas above its station; Simon Fraser, even in its infancy, appeared both trippy and corrupt; and Notre Dame in Nelson projected an airless atmosphere of conservative Catholicism which promised nothing pleasant. None offered an alternative to UBC.

But I had just taught two years at UBC, and I knew it was becoming a factory like the one I had rejected at Berkeley. In addition, teaching in the university in which one was an undergraduate requires a special kind of masochistic subservience I could never summon up. The former student never *really* becomes the

11

present colleague. He turns forty, a full professor with three books behind him, and his elders still regard him as a stripling with a certain indefinable promise.

No, I would want none of the jobs that might be available in B.C. But the decision had deeper roots, too. I have always been attracted to places passed by, to old houses falling into neglect, to projects smacking more of restoration than of innovation. My favourite part of present-day B.C. is the West Kootenays; those deep-furrowed mountain valleys ballasted by huge, clear lakes; those old towns remembering the glories of two generations ago when the mineral rushes were still in progress; the crystalline glaciers and the meadows where wild horses roam; the back roads speckled with abandoned cabins and the shacks of subsistence farmers. The one place in B.C. that I would really like to live for a while is the Novai Pasolick, the new village built by the radical Doukhobors I taught as children years ago.

And yet there is no ocean in the West Kootenays, and I can hardly imagine being happy away from salt water. For a Maritimer, a Newfoundlander, a coastal British Columbian, the sea is a route to all the world, a promise of adventure, a source of wonder and mystery, a perpetual prospect of liberation. So I came to the Maritimes, and to the gradual realization that I am in harmony with the Maritime outlook as I never was in harmony with the attitudes of B.C.

Part of the charm of my native province, after all, is its assumption that things are opening out, the world is getting better, and that death itself is little more than an illusion to be mocked by the sun-browned bodies on the beaches. That lovely sense of possibility gives B.C. people the ability to carry out astonishing projects: to dam rivers, create instant universities, knock down mountains and get rich overnight. I appreciate that quality, and I suspect Maritimers could profit from a little more such faith in their own possibilities.

But I remember the Nova Scotia painter Alex Colville—that eerie genius—remarking acerbically on "what I regard as the fatuous optimism that tends to prevail on the West Coast," and contrasting that outlook with Nova Scotian attitudes. "*Bad* things have happened here," Colville said. "Nova Scotians have the sense of progress, or change, as often being *loss.* Now I think this is simply true. One of the main features of human experience is that a lot of things actually happen for the worse.''

Colville is right—and what has happened to the Lower Mainland in the last twenty years, that explosive growth down to the American border and up the Fraser Valley to Abbotsford and Chilliwack, has happened for the worse. As an environment for people, metropolitan Vancouver is now little better than Toronto, and in some respects it is not as good. I have friends in Vancouver, university-educated people in early middle age, making what appear to be good incomes, who have to take their children and go live with their parents because they cannot find housing at a price they can pay. That, it seems to me, is genuine squalor, compared with which rural Nova Scotia is rich. Even the poorest of Cape Breton families can usually find some kind of a shanty to live in, with a patch of ground where the children can play.

And yet Maritimers are generally incredulous when I say that I'm from B.C., and I live down east by choice. Why would I live *here*? Isn't B.C. prosperous, scenic, dynamic and expansive?

Yes, I concede, it is all those things and more. But there are other values, too, of which B.C. knows nothing: the values of stability and rootedness, the sense of belonging to a well-defined community, the gentler, domesticated beauty of farmstead and fishing harbour. The sense that things are not altogether transient, that the idiosyncratic old home that has been there 200 years will not have been trampled by a high-rise developer tomorrow. The Maritimes have their own illusions, of course, but those illusions seem to me closer to the kind of thinking we will all need as the Industrial Revolution transforms itself into something less profligate, wasteful and greedy.

If I were a native Maritimer, probably I would not see it that way. Instead of stability, I would see stagnation; instead of tradition, I would see rigidity; instead of durability, decay.

If I were a native Maritimer and I saw things that way, I would probably move to B.C. Every year, hundreds of Maritimers make the long trek west to what Ross Flemington, the late Ombudsman of New Brunswick, once called "the other Maritime province." I understand completely why they flock to that enchanted land where the mountains of gold meet the sunshot sea, and I fancy that some of them may stand someday where I once did, at the forestry lookout which crowns Mount Idaho, on the edge of the Slocan Valley. I stood and looked westward, where the sun was declining over range after range of peaks and ridges and glaciers, the sky above me huge and round as a prairie sky, the view opening upon miles and miles of gaunt, torn pinnacles thrusting up endlessly on every side, clear to the horizon.

It was perhaps the most awesome natural scene I have ever seen, and as the sun dipped towards the invisible sea, it washed the panorama with the colour of its dying glory. A prodigious, extravagant splendour of mountains—and the mountains were of gold.

Savage Harbour
Prince Edward Island
July, 1977

The Iron Road to Yesterday and Tomorrow

"Capitalism is a philosophy," said the sleeping car porter. "What it is really, capitalism is an attitude towards your fellow man."

Rail passenger services, said Jean Marchand, then Transport Minister in June, 1975, should pay their own way. His successor, Otto Lang, agrees. He told the House of Commons the following January that services should be commercially viable and that fares should be set through market forces. Never mind Pierre Trudeau, who says the market economy doesn't work.

"Inflation," declared the porter, "they talk about inflation. It's always been inflation for the poor man. Whatever it cost, you couldn't afford it. Now it's hitting the middle classes, so you see it on television all the time." He's a strikingly handsome man,

big, astute and observant. He runs a bookstore on the side and is, says one of his colleagues, "big in Black Power."

Otto Lang says he's going to revitalize the passenger services. That's Ottawa doublespeak: what he really proposes is to shut most of them down. One transcontinental line, and improved services from Quebec City to Windsor, where most of the voters live. If people persist in living in places like Nova Scotia and Manitoba, well, you can't actually *stop* them. But you don't have to encourage them, either.

"You ought to write a good exposé of the CPR," suggested the club car steward. "Man, I'd love to see that."

"Who's gonna *buy* it?" demanded the porter. "How you gonna do it? Pierre Berton didn't even get into the CPR archives."

"That right?"

"That's right. He didn't have much to say about all the Chinese that got killed building the railway, either."

On a windswept December morning, my lady and I boarded the train in Cape Breton, in a shoebox of a station squatting by an Atlantic harbour; we left it in Vancouver, where the train creeps into town past freighters just in from Japan. The railway line leads into Canada's history, art, politics, literature and economics. Study the railways and you learn about our people.

The Budd car was almost full, and we found a double seat immediately behind the driver's compartment, where we could look ahead down the track as one can in a subway. We trundled over the Canso Causeway and began to feel uncomfortable. We were warm. We were hot. We were *roasting*: could we move? The conductor scowled. We wouldn't find two seats together, he said, best we should stay where we were. But the temperature must have been 33° (or 90°) and I was down to my sticky undershirt. We would move.

No, said the steward, we couldn't have *that* seat; that was where he sat when he was not dispensing fatal coffee and glutinous pre-wrapped sandwiches. We persevered, and found a cooler seat. "Take your hat checks!" barked the conductor, and snatched them out of the wall.

Not an auspicious beginning.

The other passengers smiled furtively at us, like pupils beaming support to a child being unjustly scolded.

To Antigonish, that Scotch Catholic university town, and on to the industrial glumness of New Glasgow, where the oldest locomotive in Canada lives: the mining engine *Samson*, brought to Canada in 1839. Then Truro at mid-day, and the connection with the famous CN mainliner, the *Ocean Limited*, the subject of a painting by Alex Colville and for generations the main conduit for Maritime emigration. Every day, the *Ocean Limited* traces the route of the old Intercolonial Railway, the road built by Sandford Fleming, the Canadian engineer whose railway work led him to develop the world-wide system of Standard Time.

Canada is to a large extent the *creation* of the railways, and not just the CPR. The completion of the Intercolonial, from Halifax to Montreal, was one of the terms on which Confederation itself was negotiated. It was built along the North Shore of New Brunswick for military reasons: the new nation feared an American attack.

But what is being attacked now is an acceptable lunch, as the train slides out of Truro in a thin broth of blowing snow. We are paired with a plump, cheerful Acadienne on her way home to Moncton to see her family; she has, she smiles over her Cold Duck, ten brothers and sisters, twenty-four nieces and nephews. Beside her is a peppery young woman who is probably nudging eighty, and who lights a Peter Jackson, orders a beer, and tells us that the Joseph Howe Home for Senior Citizens in Halifax is just wonderful.

"I have my own little apartment," she marvels, "and whoever designed it was thinking about senior citizens. The cupboards aren't away up there, they're down here where I can reach them. And I can afford it. My grand-daughter has a two-bedroom apartment at $400 a month—it's sky-high—but if you want a decent place where there's no rats, you got to pay it."

The waiter tries to take her half-empty plate. Swift as a hawk she clamps a hand on the plate.

"No you don't!" she cries. "I'm a slow eater, that's all."

We have a "bedroom," about eight feet long and five feet

wide, what was once considered luxury, with its own little toilet. Our porter looks a lot like Bill Downey, but that's absurd: Downey used to be a porter but he now owns The Arrows Club, the soul-music nightclub in Halifax.

Over the border into New Brunswick, reading *Strong Poison*, a Dorothy Sayers mystery. Through Sackville, that odd mixture of foundries and scholarship, and into the marshalling yards of Moncton as the light fades. We wander to the club car and fall into conversation with an expressive, indefinably stylish man who works for the Community Improvement Corporation in Bathurst. Tony Gallant comes from nearby Rogersville, but he worked for eight years in Winnipeg, Quebec and the north. His English is lilting and expressive, but he's losing his vocabulary; these days, he speaks almost entirely French.

The North Shore is anything but quaint; a succession of squalid mill towns on a bald, low shoreline, with the worst poverty and unemployment in a hard-times province. Yet its people are not sullen or cowed: they are rebellious, comical, comradely, vital. The air service here is minimal, the roads are shocking, the train is still the best route from Moncton on. These facts speak eloquently of the provincial government's neglect, and perhaps as a consequence the North Shore has the best-organized, most radical, rural poor in the Maritimes. It's a couple of years since I was there. How are the North Shore Forestry Syndicate and the *Conseil Régional d'Aménagement du Nord*? How are their people, Michel, Barney, Père Savoie? Is the local political party, the *Parti Acadien*, making any headway?

"There could be an explosion this winter, I think," says Tony. "But it could be like '73, too, a big Day of Concern and a lot of promises, but no real change. It's a question of the, ah–I don't know the English word, an–*sensibilization de la population*. That takes a long time."

And it's easy to lose hope.

"Yes, sure. Sometimes I get so discouraged I just feel like saying, the hell with it, and go off in the woods somewhere and build a little shack and stay there. Lots of people feel that now. People say, The cost of electricity is going up, oil is up, food is up; and they don't understand what's going on. You know? They can't figure it out."

Last call for dinner! Last call for dinner!

Tony sits with us briefly, shakes hands as the train crawls into Bathurst. The train threw us together, the train pulls us apart. May we meet again.

Margo orders roast beef, I order liver and bacon, and we decide on a half-bottle of cheap rosé, a total of $13.00. The train fumes in front of another graceless little example of CN modern architecture, and I gaze out at the snow, remembering a farewell at this station, parting from a friend I never saw again. I feel like a 'forties' movie.

The waiter is a young man named Deveau; he's missing a thumb, and he looks like a street-fighter from east Montreal, but the name is Acadian and in fact he comes from Yarmouth. Yes, he knows Frenchy's Used Clothing; he shops there all the time. "I'm not gonna pay $31.00 for a pair of pants; I'll take $5.00 to Frenchy's and get four whole outfits."

To bed, in the upper berth: the train is no place for lovers, even in first class. I pick up *Strong Poison* again. "I'm told I make love rather nicely," Lord Peter Wimsey is saying, "only I'm at a disadvantage at the moment." Quite, my lord. The *Ocean Limited* rocks rhythmically, click-clacking over the rails, rushing through the night towards Quebec...

The train gives a sudden jolting lurch, and stops. Five-thirty in the morning–6.30 Atlantic Time–praise Sandford Fleming. The sign says Lévis, Quebec. The looming lights across the river would be Quebec City. We're Deveau's first customers in the diner, tucking into a breakfast in the dark.

The best he can make in Yarmouth is $2.35 an hour, he says, and on the train he gets $4.37, plus his tips, and his room and lodging thrown in. It's a good deal, but in the fourteen months he's been married–proudly he shows us the fuzzy snapshot of a pretty girl–he's had maybe two months at home. "We want a house," he explains, "and we're sacrificing a lot, but what can you do?" Margo mentions the rumours that Trudeau will wipe out transcontinental passenger service, and Deveau is horrified. "If he does that he kills Canada at the same time." But he expects that the two railways will be merged, and predicts service from Halifax to Montreal in fourteen hours on a brand-new roadbed.

19

The *Ocean Limited* is perhaps twenty-one hours from Halifax now as it pulls into the station in the bowels of Montreal, deep below the Queen Elizabeth Hotel. It's 8.30 in the morning. The porter stops me in the passageway.

"Don't I know you?" he asks.

"I was thinking you look a lot like Bill Downey."

"I *am* Bill Downey, that's why!"

"I thought you'd have quit the trains now you've got The Arrows?"

"I got twenty-five years with the railroad," says Bill, "and I want that pension. So how you been?"

We transfer to Windsor Station, a couple of blocks away, where we'll switch to Canadian Pacific for the trip west. It's drizzling rain, and outside the Château Champlain, where we repair for another micro-breakfast, the red Christmas lights on the potted trees look slightly silly and forlorn, like sodden wrapping paper.

At 11.15 we board the *Canadian*, which for some inexplicable reason is waiting far down the platform, well outside the cover of the station roof. With winter clothes and luggage, on a still, humid day, the trek to the train is no pleasure. It was hot in the Budd car, hot in last night's "bedroom," and now it is hot again inside the heavy overcoat. We clamber aboard, and almost at once the train slips forward. Up to the dome car to see Montreal pass by.

How is the train shrunk!

The last time I crossed the country by rail, in 1964, I was going the other way, heading for Europe on a train which even then seemed short. Today it's only a perfunctory gesture: six cars, two of them dome cars. Eleven years ago I took the *Dominion*, which no longer exists, a more leisurely train which consumed an extra day and stopped in all kinds of little places. That was why I took it: I had always lived west of the Rockies, and I wanted to see with my own eyes the sweep of the Prairies, the rock and muskeg of northwestern Ontario, the rim of Lake Superior.

The train's chief entertainments are reading, talking, and gorging. If the railways wanted passengers, they'd offer more: first-run movies, playrooms for the kids, game rooms, conference rooms, taped commentaries on the passing scenery, bridal suites, casinos, live music. The possibilities are endless, and no imagination has been applied to them for at least a generation. Instead, the service has been allowed to slide into a genteel tackiness, like an old wino with the manners of a gentleman.

Consider the diner now as we diesel through the farmlands of the lower Ottawa Valley. The *maître de* is mottled and wattled, with liverish spots on his talons and a sallow complexion. He is both charming and efficient, whisking you into a seat, holding the chair, able to cope gracefully with the exigencies of a crowded, swaying restaurant.

But the restaurant contains only the two of us, and a brace of elderly Americans. We're outnumbered by the staff.

The waiter himself is also a survivor from the glory days, and a credit to his calling. Unlike the people's railway, the CPR still has cloth and silver on the table; the sugar is not in those ubiquitous paper envelopes, but in sterling bowls. "Ah, those bags, they're coming," confides the waiter, with a resigned Quebec shrug. "But I only got ten months to go to retirement, I hope I won't be here to see them."

It's like a scene from some sad and absurd film, this diner full of old men with nothing to do, full of knowledge and experience and flair, serving cheeseburgers with little plastic bags of Kraft relish and mustard on the side. Our waiter has been with the CPR for forty-five years. He's never learned to drive a car: between the trains, the buses, the taxis and the Métro of his native Montreal, he's never needed one. Union Pacific, Penn Central–they all honoured his pass–and he travelled all over the continent on them.

"The railways never came back after the war," he says. "Before the war, cars were for the rich; afterwards, everybody could have them–my sons, my daughter–but before the war, the train was the way you travelled. There were *twelve* dining cars going out of Montreal every day then, *twelve*, heading in every direction. Now there's one."

"Well, the train's too slow for young people. I have a friend, he drives to Sudbury in five and a half hours. It takes eleven hours by train." Sure, but on the train you can read, talk–you

21

don't have to grip the wheel and concentrate on not getting killed. "I agree, I agree," he says, "but most people wouldn't spend the extra time."

We finish our cheeseburgers in the new Ottawa station–a single station serving both railways–a forerunner of Otto Lang's future. The old station downtown is a conference hall these days, across from the Château Laurier. Squinting out the window, I can just make out the Peace Tower on the skyline. I suppose this glass-and-steel cube makes sense; certainly it's better than the little plastic boxes of Bathurst and Port Hawkesbury. But when the train no longer delivers you downtown, it's lost a big advantage over an airplane.

Up the Ottawa Valley, the first time I ever saw it in daylight. Old brick towns, progressively less spacious and charming as the train pushes north and west. Arnprior: water and dun brick and the warm tones of a falling sun. Someday I will go to Arnprior to talk and prowl and learn, for to Arnprior in the early years of the last century came an immigrant from Inverness, Scotland, named Alexander O'Kain Cameron, and he was my grandfather's grandfather, but I have never visited his town.

Renfrew, Pembroke, Chalk River at dusk. Town of atomic scientists, a mysterious place one views with the mingled dread and admiration which mediaeval man probably reserved for alchemists. Reading and then dining as Moor Lake and Bass Lake and Deux Rivières flip past, route of the voyageurs, and Mattawa:

"Big Joe Mufferaw paddled into Mattawa
　All the way from Ottawa in just one day;
　On the River Ottawa, the best man we ever saw
　Was Big Joe Mufferaw, the old folks say–"*

Stompin' Tom's hero was quite a man, all right; it must be about two hundred miles he'd paddled. Once the song starts, you can't stop it: *Big Joe Mufferaw*, chants the internal tape recorder, *paddled into Mattawa....*

North Bay in the early evening, bitter cold and blowing snow,

*From *Stompin' Tom Connors Meets Big Joe Mufferaw*, Boot Records, Toronto.

stamping on the platform and looking at the raw, frontierish street presented by the town my father was born in. By 1907 we were a railroad family; my grandfather was a divisional accountant with the CPR, and my father grew up in Regina, Calgary and Nelson, moving like a leaf in the winds of my grandfather's job and my grandmother's health. And then later he put himself through college waiting on tables in the trains and the paddlewheel steamers the CPR used to run on Kootenay Lake. I recall as a kid being wakened by his cry, "Rise and shine for the Good Old Line!" and somehow I always imagined the Good Old Line to be the CPR. He used to tell how my Uncle Cecil worked those summers on the section gangs, and how Cece would watch for Dad's train, and as it whirled past the two brothers would wave, their only contact in a whole hot, young summer.

The trains are not mere economics and logistics; to a Canadian the trains are folklore and mythology. They are our American Revolution, our King Alfred and Robert the Bruce, our Long March, our *Satyagraha* campaigns. A queer, mechanical mythology, unquestionably, and one shot through with ironies, but the railways were indeed the national venture which formed this timorous, resilient, inchoate country. They crop up in our imaginations like an obsession. E. J. Pratt wrote an epic poem about them; Gordon Lightfoot's greatest song celebrates them; Pierre Berton has made them the basis of a one-man industrial enterprise.

The hero of Hugh MacLennan's famous novel *Barometer Rising*, waiting for a tram in Halifax one night in 1917, suddenly grasps the incredible scale of his native country, and imagines the way the sunlight falls on its unbelievable breadth. "The railway line," he thinks, "that tenuous thread which bound Canada to both the great oceans and made her a nation, lay with one end in the darkness of Nova Scotia and the other in the flush of a British Columbian noon." Stephen Leacock's finest book begins and ends with a railway journey. Canadian writers get as excited about trains as French writers do about sex. I'm not immune myself.

At bedtime we are shunting in Sudbury, picking up the cars from Toronto, and during the night we pass through Chapleau, where the author of *Maria Chapdelaine*, Louis Hémon, was

23

killed by a train in 1913. History, history. This part of the line is not as dramatic as the Rockies, but it was perhaps the most disheartening to build, blasting through bedrock and sinking in muskeg. It reminds you, too, of how enormous Ontario actually is. The urban southeast imposes itself on the mind as "Ontario," but in the morning we are just in Schreiber, at noon in Thunder Bay, and only as the third day's travel ends do we approach the Manitoba border.

The crew changes at Winnipeg, and I say my good-byes from the station, where I am phoning my aunt, for my mother's family commences now and is scattered like tumbleweed over the Prairies. The railway was to open the West, and two of the people who flowed through the opening were my great-grandfathers Robertson and Flack who took up farms near a branch line west of Winnipeg, relying on the CPR and cursing it at the same time. There's a famous story about a farmer whose crops had failed, whose animals had died, whose equipment had broken down and whose mortgage had been foreclosed. He got home from town to find his wife had run off with the hired man. He walked into a field, shook his fist at the sky, and shouted, "GOD DAMN THE CPR!!!" I don't think I'm related to him by blood, but I might be.

For if the CPR opened the West, it also held it by the throat for decades, parlaying its government-guaranteed monopoly into one of the largest concentrations of corporate power in the world. It started in 1881 with $25 million, and 25 million acres of land. That gave it the right to establish cities, of which it would own the downtowns–Regina, Calgary, Vancouver. Airlines, oil wells, steamships, pipelines, mines, forest products, hotels, smelters–CP is into them all. *Intercorporate Ownership*, the government publication, takes two pages just to list the CPR's holdings. Within a few years it's expected to be among the half-dozen largest pools of wealth in the world. And the whole empire was built on the backs of people like my grandfathers, on the sweat of Irish navvies and the blood of Chinese coolies, on the tax money that in 1975 provided $93 million in subsidies to a company which likes to paint itself as a triumph of "free" enterprise. To love the trains and loathe Canadian Pacific: that's the birth-mark of a Westerner.

Brandon at bedtime, and across from the station is a church with an onion-domed steeple, looking as strange and exotic under the wide sky of the plains as a pagoda, another memorial to the *pot-pourri* of immigrants who settled the West. We cover most of Saskatchewan during the night, rising to greet another bright dawn in Maple Creek, just outside the Alberta border.

From Montreal to Winnipeg the train was a hollow shell: one or two silent observers in the dome cars, a few bored mothers in the sleeping cars, nobody at all in the club car but Artie, the steward. Artie was perhaps the high point of the entire trip, a trim and good-humoured man of forty-eight who looked a good twenty years younger, who was delighted to discover that I too loved the great swing bands.

"How 'bout Basie? You like Basie?"

"Goodman was my favourite. But I like Basie, yeah."

"Goodman, yeah. Basie's good, though. Not as good as Ellington. Basie says that himself, he ain't the Duke. After the war I used to see all those guys in Vancouver at that club—*aaah*! I can't remember the name—but you couldn't buy a drink there then, you had to bring your own bottle. They had Ellington, Hampton—"

"The Cave?"

"The *Cave*, right! Hey, you know what's coming to Montreal next month? Oscar Peterson and Ella Fitzgerald on a double bill. Man, I can't wait for that."

Another man came in, and the steward receded a bit. Jack was in his fifties, wearing a suit jacket, check pants and a sport shirt. He works in the CPR yard in Thunder Bay, he'd just been down to Ottawa to visit his married daughter. His grandchildren were in a Christmas pageant, so he'd gone to church for the first time in twenty years. "Imagine that," he chuckled. "Travelling a thousand miles to go to church." We talked about the transition from steam to diesel, about how the huge engines are maintained, about how one keeps track of all those boxcars—not surprisingly, they're all remembered by a computer.

25

"Sure there's a market for rail travel," he said. "The railways could be drawing the passengers if they'd advertise, but they won't. They want *out* of the passenger business."

"That's right," echoed Artie. "Let the whole thing run down so nobody uses it, then they can get out of it. Look at this car. Now this car was built in 1955. It should have been renovated or replaced years ago. But they just let it go."

It's true: the rolling stock is distinctly down-at-heel. Like a 'fifties' hotel, it's old enough to be grubby but not old enough to be campy.

An elderly American woman, jowly, blue-rinsed, her hand aglitter with rocks, subsided into a seat, seized the conversation like a recalcitrant child and shook the life out of it. Her husband is a retired admiral, but "he was a railway buff before he was a sea buff," and so she's travelled on trains all over the world–this was her fifth trip this year on the CPR alone. "They call him the Admiral of the CPR now," she declared, "We know everyone on these trains." Artie faded into the woodwork, utterly silent. She has two sons-in-law on nuclear submarines, and "I've had the thrill of firing an atomic missile on a nuclear sub," she laughed. "Of course there was no missile in the tube. They take them out at the wharf, and then if you have security clearance you can go aboard."

Her sons-in-law are fine, clean-cut boys, who went through Annapolis. "You get a good class of boys there, oh, there's the odd bad apple, but the boys usually weed them out themselves, you can't haze 'em out any more, if you give 'em fifty pushups you have to do 'em too. But the boys have their ways..."

"The old silent treatment," smiled Jack, with a wink to me.

"Where are *you* going?" she demanded.

"Vancouver," I conceded.

"I've been there many times, I like it *very* much. I think they've gotten over the worst of their hippiedom. A couple of years ago I was looking out of our room in the Georgian Towers and I saw a couple of these unwashed idiots–idiots, that's what I call them, that's what they are–" she spit, "and they were pouring soap in the fountain. I called the desk. The fountain was just *foaming*, there were soap bubbles ten stories up in the air–''

I burst out laughing.

"You think that's *funny*, do you?" she glared, sweeping her eyes over my longish hair.

"Well, yes."

"It took a man two days to clean it up. I don't call that funny. You wouldn't if you were paying the bill."

"I guess we're all paying the bill," said Jack, with a wry grin. "But it's only a prank."

"Parasites," scowled the Admiral's lady. "I call anyone who costs the public money, *parasites*."

"We're all in trouble, then," I said, "considering that this train is 80 per cent subsidized."

She raged on about the iniquities of welfare people in Charleston, where she now lives. That sounded to me like a covert way of damning the blacks, and I stole a glance at Artie. His face was utterly impassive.

The Admiral's lady is the opposite side of Tony Gallant: the train lets you talk, but if you don't want to talk with someone you have precious little place to hide. First-class, however, confers options unknown to coach travellers. I got up as though to seek a toilet, and instead retired to the "bedroom" and Lord Peter Wimsey, leaving Margo to the mercies of Charleston's ambassador. Sometimes one does terrible things to one's best friends.

Next day we dodged the Admiral, a pleasant old rogue except that he regarded the rest of the world as composed of junior officers, and talked again with Artie. A sleeping car porter joined us, and they reminisced about the auctions when the CPR rid itself of the old private cars, the silver, the spittoons, including R.B. Bennett's spittoon.

"Oh, he was tight!" cried Artie. "Tight with his own money, tight with the government's. He travelled all over on the CPR, always in an upper berth."

"That's right," said the porter. "He took a spittoon with him into the berth and used it for a chamber pot, he had weak kidneys. Porter wouldn't be looking for it, of course; likely as not he'd get it all over him."

They mentioned company discipline. Artie missed a train once, and got ten demerit points. Sixty and you're fired, but you can retrieve twenty a year. Drinking on the job is forty-five points. "And womanizing is instant dismissal – I've seen a lot of good men fired for that."

"How'd they get caught?" asked Margo.

"Conductor would walk the whole length of the train, and if he heard anything suspicious, it was, *All right, you, come on out.*"

"Aw, just five minutes more," pleaded Margo.

"No five minutes, get out now. Out here."

"Two minutes."

"No two minutes either, come out, come out."

"Sixty seconds? Just sixty seconds?"

"You come out here, buddy, just the way you are, pants or no pants," ordered Artie, shaking his head. "Lots of those guys were married men, too. How would they explain it to their wives?"

"Gee, honey," I said, "she told me she had bedbugs in there, I was just checking the mattress...."

"Without your *pants*?" cried Artie.

We rode the locomotive, which is strictly Not Allowed, for 150 miles. Like so many others, the engineer, Matthew, is preparing for retirement after the best part of fifty years on the railway. He began in the office, became a wiper, a fireman in 1938, an engineer in 1945. Leaving the station, he cracked open the throttle: the engines wound up, and the train glided forward. The big diesels actually drive huge generators, which in turn drive electric motors on the wheels. A far cry from the old steamers with their coaling bunkers and water tanks?

"Oh, I could write a book about steam!" chuckled Matthew. "We used to shovel twenty-five ton o' coal on this run. I wish I had a penny for every ton o' coal I've shovelled. I spent most o' me time with me ass to the moon. And all kinds of things to go wrong: a poor grade o' coal, a leaky boiler, the front end plugged up with snow. You really felt like you muscled the train down the track in them days."

The train cruised nicely at 70, but most of the time we were down around 50 to 55. Hills and curves slow her down, and it takes two miles to get the speed down from 70 to 50, using a big brake handle for the train as a whole, a little one for the engine itself. You have to brake on the way up a hill to get the effect going down. Along the track were lines of orange fires: old railway ties, replaced during the summer but burnt only after snow flew.

"Now here," said Matthew, "this is a section you can only do 45. The ties are rotten—they've probably been down since '28 or '29—and when the train goes over them the spikes pull out, the plates start jumpin', even the rails begin to move. They were supposed to be replaced this year, but it didn't get done.

"Funny thing, there's still nothin' for railway ties as good as jackpine. They've tried everything else—concrete, hardwood, you name it—but nothin' stands up as good as jackpine."

A bell started ringing, like a fire alarm: a malfunction in the engine somewhere, and Harry the fireman went to check it. We rode on, the green lights flicking on every couple of miles to signal that the track ahead was empty. Matthew got on the radio every now and then, checking the progress of Number Two, the eastbound version of the *Canadian*. It loomed up out of the forest, raising a dust-storm of snow, its big headlight blazing in the afternoon like a giant white eye.

"Where you been?" radioed Matthew.

"Comin', comin'," crackled the radio.

Zip-zip-zip, and Number Two was gone.

"They were late yesterday, too," Matthew explained, "because of a mishap." That means a wreck, right? "Right." Do they have many wrecks? Matthew shrugged. "As long as there's railroads there'll be wrecks. Mostly they aren't very serious."

The cab is like a ship's engine room: dirty paint on metal bulkheads, everything strictly functional, a cooler full of cold tinned drinking water. A roar of GM V-16 diesels washed Harry back through the bulkhead door. "You wanna see the engines?" he asked. You bet.

The train is pulled by two locomotives, back to back. The bell was a traction motor on one of the wheels; it had burned out, but it didn't affect our progress. These locomotives were twenty-five years old, veterans of God knows how many transcontinental crossings, 1850 horsepower each. We passed through a cramped and roaring space, Harry explaining at the top of his voice, and then he opened a door. I was looking outside. We crossed the swaying platform between the two locomotives and entered the roar again, then went back to the deserted cab of the second engine, facing backwards. The noise subsided.

"You never know who you're gonna find in here," Harry laughed. "You know, fairly often you come back and there's some hobo stretched out in here having a snooze or something." I didn't know that still went on. "It's not like the 'thirties, but it still goes on." Do any bigwigs ever come and ride up front? Harry laughed again. "Only *little* bigwigs."

Back in the cab, Matthew talked about accidents. Once he nearly hit another train himself. "They were replacing steel, and a freight stalled on the crossing back to the westbound track. I came up on him at 60, but I had the brake set; I was able to stop two car-lengths behind him. They were relyin' on the radio and the radio wasn't workin' good. The brakeman should have been another thirty-five or forty power poles behind, flaggin'. Dumb bugger."

And once a woman died under his engine. They stopped for two minutes in a small town, and she came out of an alleyway and lay down on the tracks. "We didn't hear nothin'. Not a scream, not a peep. We didn't know a thing about it till a westbound train met us and told us on the radio fifteen miles later. Didn't feel too good about it. Apparently she'd tried it three or four times before. Cut her right in two." He pointed at the floor. "She just lay down right under there."

If he had it to do again, would he choose to work on the trains? He thought about it for a moment, turning the idea around.

"Yeah," he said slowly, "I think so. An old-timer said to me once, and I think it's true, there's never a day goes by on this job you don't learn something. You know? You learn something every day. That counts for a lot."

We flattened ourselves against the bulkhead as Matthew pulled into his home town, "just in case some bugger's in the station lookin' out.'' Then a scramble down the high steel side of the locomotive, a hurried and furtive farewell, and back to the club car through the steam.

"What was it like?" asked Artie, with eager curiosity. "You know, in twenty-eight years on the trains, I've never had a ride in a locomotive?"

Waking in Saskatchewan, the flatland flying by, the images of three days on the train passing in review: the man in Nova Scotia chopping a hole in the ice, the abandoned hayrick with its fallen load covered in snow in New Brunswick, the towers of Montreal, snow-blowers on the airstrip at Thunder Bay, a plane on a frozen lake near Kenora, a Buick keeping pace with the train in a snowstorm.

Breakfast in Medicine Hat, the train stopping to move passengers from a coach which had broken a water pipe and flooded, staring at sparrows on the roadbed and the face of the Assiniboia Inn. An antelope skittering on the hills just outside the town. On across the Prairies, the endless lines of telephone poles, the widely scattered farms, the towns focused on grain elevators. Suffield, Alberta! An infamous town, though I had never known where it was: for here Canada does its research in chemical and biological warfare, ready to put nerve gas and bubonic plague to the good work of making the world safe for the likes of the CPR.

Something odd has happened: the train has filled up since Winnipeg. I meet a man bound for a vacation in Hawaii, Margo encounters a couple of long-hairs travelling on CPR passes, heading for holidays in Calgary and California. They've been drinking since they joined the train in Manitoba, they've snorted some mescaline, and they're high as clouds. Join us in the cafeteria car, man, wanna do some mesc?

One of them works on the actual roadbed, and he tells us that the rails we're riding on are a quarter of a mile long, which is why we so rarely hear the click-click of passing over a joint. But these are lousy rails, from Ontario; the really good rails come, he says, from "Newfoundland or someplace down there." From Sydney, Cape Breton, I suggest. "Right, that's the place. Now *they* make good rails. That's what CN uses.

"Funny thing about the CPR: they'll never do *anything* first.

31

Not until CN has shown it'll work. That's how CP makes money."

In the cafe car all hands are into the beer. There's Hans, a quiet young Bostonian taking the trip as an interesting way to get from Massachusetts to California; he makes a living tending a summer home for its wealthy owners. There's Andy, who looks like an overweight schoolmarm and works for the CPR. There's John, a wavy-haired young man who nods and seems pleasant, but says nothing. And there's Ronnie.

Ronnie is a CPR employee too. He's twenty-three, the single father of a six-year-old, blonde-moustached and straggly-haired, with a marijuana conviction and a deportation from the U.S. already behind him. He's drunk and impudent and vulgar and funny, already a poignant and difficult loser. "You're too old," he tells me. "You're a fucked-up hippie. So am I. How old are you, anyway? Yeah, well when *I'm* thirty-eight I'm gonna have hair down to my ass."

The conductor hears this, and scowls at him. "Look at that bastard," mutters Ronnie. "I been tryin' to buy a berth on this train all the way from Thunder Bay. He won't sell me one. I got the money, but he won' sell me a berth."

He gets into a scholarly discussion about the finer variations among Winnipeg motorcycle gangs.

"Nah, nah, you're full of shit!" he cries. "The Manitoba Angels are on'y a subsidiary of the Black Devil Riders, man. But the Spartans are the heavy ones now. I can't stand 'em, except for one guy."

"The Angels got broke up because their president took all the charges on that manslaughter thing," says Andy. "Six charges he took. He got fifteen years."

"Yeah, and that other gang, I forget their name," says Ronnie, "they got all fucked-up because their president turned out to be a narc."

"Bad scene."

"I belong to the Rebels," says Ronnie proudly. "We got together for self-protection, bunch of freaks. You know what one of our meetings was like? Sit around and do a lot of dope, drop some acid...."

"I heard you guys got only one 350 cc. Honda among ya."

32

"That's right, man. We usedta walk the streets, all thirty of us together, and this one little Honda putt-putting along beside the curb..."

They get off, most of them, at Calgary. I try to make a call to yet another uncle and aunt, but by train time I still haven't found an unoccupied phone booth in the station. I scramble aboard, and the train doesn't move. Evidently the flooded coach has to be taken off, and that takes time. We're nearly an hour late pulling out.

That hour costs us a good chunk of the Rockies, which stand now like the teeth of a saw on the western edge of the plains, visible for miles. And today we are passing through lands where the railway brought the settlers, where silent Indians rode up beside the construction crews, watched, and silently rode away. This country evokes the memories of Mounties like Colonel MacLeod, missionaries like Father Lacombe, and Indians like that noble spirit Crowfoot, through whose country we passed this morning. The urgency of their crises came from the trains themselves, symbols of onrushing history marching inexorably over the plains as Van Horne drove his vast organization day after day to reach the impossible target of 500 miles of track in a single summer. Instant cities sprang up on its route, newspapers were published, settlers fanned out to break soil. Did ever a land change so rapidly?

Cochrane. Canmore. The foothills swell and fall away, the crenellated peaks draw closer, and abruptly the train is rushing into deep clefts between peaks so high you cannot see their tops from the sleeper window. Out of the bedroom, then, for the best way to see the Rockies—and the Rockies justify all the superlatives that have been heaped on them—is from the dome car of a train. The mountains seem bent on outdoing one another—here a spike, there a plunging valley, over here a ruff of trees on the skyline. This is the high point of a continent, the waters tumbling eastward to the Atlantic, westward to the Pacific, and now, heading into the fourth night on the train, one feels a precariously balanced sense of the size and majesty of the country we have travelled, a country which even in the bleakness of mid-winter is so spectacular that it must surely determine the way Canadians

33

respond to life. No wonder Europe, for all its charm, always feels cramped and concentrated.

Ronnie sits with us, muttering outrageous opinions in pungent language, his sock feet propped up on the dashboard. The conductor bustles up.

"Get your boots on and get back in the coach where you belong. Move it, now, within two minutes, or I'll have the RCMP take you off the train at Banff."

"I'm gonna buy a berth—"

"No you're not. You aren't getting in the sleeper. Two minutes, now. We don't want your kind back here."

"What's my kind?"

"Never mind that, just get moving or off you go at Banff."

With a final jab of his finger in the kid's shoulder, the conductor marches off, choleric and self-righteous. It's funny: he seems indignant at the kid's style and his lack of rank more than anything. Something snaps into place for me: it's social class. He finds the kid an offensive nobody, and suddenly I'm angry, for the Admiral and his wife offended my values profoundly and made themselves at least as much of a nuisance as Ronnie, but *they* were treated with sickening deference by the authorities on the train. The kid's money *isn't* as good as theirs. The train is the most class-structured environment I've seen in a long, long time, and I find myself ashamed to be travelling first-class, even though I couldn't have endured the trip without the sanctuary of a private space.

Ronnie goes on muttering, assuring us that he's clean enough to stand a search, and at Banff two bulky Mounties stalk into the club car, frisk him and march him off. "Was he a bad man, Daddy?" asks a boy, and his father smiles across the car at us. "No," he replies, "he'd just had a bit too much to drink." Most passengers seem to agree that Ronnie was more a loser than a villain, and the conductor finds the atmosphere chilly enough that he tries to explain it to some of us, assuring us that Ronnie will only be held overnight in the drunk tank and put back on tomorrow's train. But it isn't merely the fact of his ejection that bothers us, it's the contemptuous manner, which can't be explained away.

By now we have passed Lake Louise, and in the gathering darkness we approach the Spiral Tunnels, a phenomenal piece of engineering. The original Big Hill roadbed was so steep that train after train ran off the rails and crashed into the canyon far below. The train now makes a complete circle twice, inside the mountain; with a train of any length, the locomotive has emerged from the mountain before the last cars have entered it at right angles above.

And now a man comes up from the baggage car. He thinks we might like to know a bit about the tunnels, built in 1908. He points out the old roadbed, which is terrifying just to observe, twice as steep as what we're on. Come over here, he says, and you can see the other end of the tunnel below us. That's Mount Stephen there, yes, and that's the Kicking Horse River.

He lives in Medicine Hat, and travels as far as Field. In the summer he brings a motorbike and goes fishing in all the lakes nearby during his layover; after his retirement he'd like to climb Mount Stephen. There's Cathedral Mountain. There's Field, B.C., down there, and I've got to go back to work. . . .

He's followed by a chorus of thanks, and there's something really touching about his gesture, sharing with us the experience of a lifetime. He makes up for the conductor.

Dinner, a good book, and lights out. During the evening we're shunted for a long while, and someone in the hall explains that we have a "hotbox," a wheel bearing which has overheated. It could seize up, twist off the wheel and derail the train, so that coach has to be left here.

During the night I wake and sit by the window for twenty minutes, smoking and watching the train wind along sandy hills beside a lake or perhaps a big river. The Thompson? The upper Fraser? When I wake again we're in Agassiz, just below the Fraser Canyon, in dense fog which has condensed as hoar frost on the leafless trees, the woods frozen into the delicate carving of a Chinese ivory fan. Down near Mission we pass a big wreck, the top of a boxcar protruding from the muddy Fraser, loose lumber corralled within a boom.

Haney, Pitt Meadows, the outstretching suburban arms of Vancouver. In the train, the bustle of people packing up, the

35

muted excitement and the queer *camaraderie* of impending arrival. The family from California laughs with the mother from Bella Coola. Port Moody, and salt water on the right now, the upper reaches of Burrard Inlet, the other ocean achieved at last.

After four nights and five days it *does* seem like an achievement, and I have certainly had enough of the train for now. Yet the train is surely the most *interesting* form of travel we have, and probably the least threatening to the environment. The trains are losing money because what they seem bent on offering is only a slow and shabby version of air travel: all that remains from their grand days are the people. The trains need to offer something different. Competing with the airlines on airline terms means the trains automatically lose.

But the trains can even be considered *economically* attractive. The passenger trains lost $167 million in 1974, but the cost of the Mirabel Airport and the Pickering Non-Airport, nearly $2 *billion*, would cover that loss for ten years. Operating costs for airports run to $600 million a year, nearly four times the loss on passenger trains; highways set us back $1.2 billion annually. Do airline and bus passengers pay their own way? Of course not; compared to railway passengers they represent a positive haemorrhage in the treasury.

Like most issues, however, the question of the trains will be resolved not by good sense, but by force of circumstance. As the cost of fuel rises, the trains will come back into their own, just as sailing ships have become a hot topic of research around the world. A train will move a lot more passengers on a gallon of fuel than a jet plane. As usual, the federal government is unbuckling just in time to be sure we're caught with our pants down. Remember those ancient days when we could afford to export virtually any amount of oil, gas and power at minimal prices? That was only five years ago, and the same lads who gave us the fuel shortage are still minding the shop.

Slower and slower. We are looking at the backs of warehouses and the bows of freighters. It's Vancouver, downtown Vancouver, itself a creation of the railway. The *Canadian* eases into the old station at the foot of Granville Street, where I used to go as a child to meet my aunt arriving on the *Kettle Valley*, a train long since faded into memory, whose locomotives had huge wheels and pulled into the station wreathed in steam.

Vancouver. Ocean to ocean. And John Newlove's poem:

"The locomotive in the city's distance, obscure, misplaced, sounds a child's horn on the flat land leading to the cliff of dark buildings,

the foghorns on the water's edge cry back....
History, history!"*

(May, 1976)

---

*From "The Engine and the Sea" in *The Fat Man*, McClelland and Stewart Limited, 1977, p. 76. Reproduced by permission.

The Fighter in the Fishery:

Madame Edna Landry, proprietor of the diner in Petit de Grat, Nova Scotia, says that Homer Stevens "was the best damn thing that ever happened in this town. And you can go up and tell that turncoat priest I said so."

Father Georges Arsenault, the priest in question, says that Homer Stevens made him "awfully scared." If Stevens' United Fishermen and Allied Workers' Union had won the 1970 Canso Strait trawlermen's strike, "he'd be running the whole labour movement in eastern Nova Scotia today."

A. L. Cadegan, who managed Acadia Fisheries' two plants in Canso and Mulgrave, Nova Scotia, before the company went bankrupt, says that Homer Stevens is "a goddam Communist"

A PORTRAIT OF

HOMER
STEVENS

38

who "almost destroyed" the Nova Scotia fishery.

A union fisherman in the beer parlour of Vancouver's shabby Patricia Hotel says Homer Stevens is "one of the greatest men that ever lived in this country."

An executive in a Vancouver fishing company, flatly refusing to be identified, says "some of our management just throw up their hands at the mention of his name."

And on Friday, November 5, 1971, at about 10.20 AM, Homer Stevens himself says that he would like a little of that Lamb's Palm Breeze Light Rum, and no more insults about his stomach ulcer. Steering the halibut longliner *Phyllis Cormack*–better known as *Greenpeace I*–around Vancouver's inner harbour, Stevens leads a noisy flotilla of thirty-odd fishboats protesting the American nuclear test slated for Amchitka Island, in a demonstration arranged jointly by the union and the Don't Make A Wave Committee. On this raw, gusty morning, Homer Stevens is cold.

"Tell them," he calls to Don Taylor, president of the Vancouver local, who is talking by radio to a TV station, "that we're going to stop as close to the U.S. Consulate as we can get and all blow our whistles."

All morning the *Greenpeace* will receive and discharge cameramen and recording technicians, newsmen and columnists. Stevens will be cordial, obliging, serious and articulate. The union has always taken a position against nuclear testing as part of its general stand against war, he will explain, the wind ruffling his spiky black hair and grey mutton chops. But obviously the prospect that this particular test may have serious effects on the North Pacific fishery makes it unusually threatening for commercial fishermen. Well, in one form or another the union goes back about sixty years. No, it has never undertaken a demonstration quite like this before.

The demonstration is fully covered by all the media.

"If there had been any goddam run of dog salmon out there, Nick," Stevens declares to a Ladner fisherman the next day, "every little kite that could have floated would have been out there yesterday. They might not have been out there the day before, when it was howlin' fifty miles an hour, but don't

39

horseshit me that they wouldn't have been–"

"Yeah, but Homer, to get there by 10.00 o'clock I–"

"Christ, Bert Ogden left at 4.00 o'clock in the morning from Nanaimo with four fishermen aboard and a couple of their wives."

"Yeah, well if you had a good boat possibly you could make it across, but–"

"It's not like the west coast of Vancouver Island, for Christ's sake, it's–"

"This time o' the year," interjects Nick, "you don't go across in that little floating coffin of mine. (*Oh, ho, ho*, scoffs Homer.) No sir, last year when everybody's heading for the Gulf I head in, you know, I–"

"Well, I looked in vain for the Ladner local, I'll put it that way," says Homer, sorting through some papers. "I'm sure one boat in Ladner could have floated around there somehow, even if it went backwards. Look, this is Massey's copy...."

When I phoned from the east, Stevens had thought Monday would be a good time to get together, but on Monday he was in Ottawa. Tuesday night he was back, and at 9.00 the next morning I parked outside the Fisherman's Hall at 138 East Cordova Street, in a scruffy no-man's-land between Chinatown's neon restaurants, the pop history of Gastown, and the industrial slums of the East End. Across the street from the Harbour Light Salvation Army Mission, the union hall, a dark, newish building, seems to be hunched against the perpetually pelting rain.

In the third-floor office, general organizer Walter Ironside flirts harmlessly with the secretaries, like a grizzled teddy bear. Homer will be in, he says, but he has been held up by a bad accident on the Oak Street bridge. The office sports a poster from the Montreal-based radical monthly *Last Post*, a tin labelled Give To The Children of Vietnam, a chalked sign: *AMCHITKA PROTEST. Greenpeace No. 1 will lead flotilla of boats....* A poster exhorts me to Free Angela. An anti-Amchitka petition on the counter invites Canada to steer its trade to non-testing nations, to end the Defence Production Sharing Agreement, to withdraw from NORAD and to resist the continental energy scheme. I sign it. Still no sign of Homer Stevens.

Don Taylor comes in, huge in his sheepskin jacket. Walter asks him if he's getting any boats together for the demonstration. Working on it, Don says. "Be very embarrassing if we couldn't put some boats behind it, wouldn't it?"

By 9.30 welfare director Buck Suzuki is on the phone in his office, and business agent Glen McEachern comes over to say that Homer has a committee meeting at 9.30 and a herring negotiation at 10.30, so he won't have time to do more than arrange a meeting today. About quarter to ten a tall, quiet, rather gaunt-looking man appears in the outer office: Homer Stevens. His handshake, like his voice, is extraordinarily soft, as though he were totally devoid of aggression. He is not, of course: his intensities burn out at you from his glittering X-ray eyes. Even in terrible old newspaper photographs, those eyes bore into yours, penetrating, unnerving: the eyes of a hypnotist or a shaman. No wonder his enemies yap like foamy-mouthed terriers when they talk of him, for while his voice is all sweet reason, his eyes, perched up there on his Indian's cheekbones, hint at knowledge, at will, at power.

But this Wednesday morning we are only, thank God, arranging to meet. Perhaps Friday, after the *Greenpeace* demonstration? Sure, and can I go along Friday? Of course, just talk to Don Taylor. Fleetingly, Stevens seems a trifle uncertain about the whole notion of an article on him. Like any good Marxist, he believes in the power of people's movements, class consciousness, the tides of history. Even the most gifted leader is finally not very important.

And of course he is largely right: the United Fishermen is more than Homer Stevens, and he cannot lead men where they are unwilling to go. For just this reason, I am listening carefully to the men around him – Hal Griffin, for instance – to whose office I now repair. Griffin edits the union newspaper, *The Fisherman*, a punchy and well-written fortnightly which mixes factual stories about the industry, social news like that of a country weekly, and information about labour, race, war and economics from all over the world in a conscious effort to "link up what Canadian fishermen face with the struggles of oppressed people all over the world," as Stevens puts it.

41

At fifty-nine, Hal Griffin is "a poet," he says dryly, "better known in the Soviet Union than in Canada." A slight, thoughtful and generous man, he was formerly editor of the *Pacific Tribune*. He is a very good journalist—his *British Columbia: The People's Early History* deftly tells a very different story from the one I learned in the B.C. schools—and I admire the devotion to his principles which has led him to slug it out most of his life on obscure left-wing papers. Though his willingness to justify the Czech and Hungarian invasions bothers me, I find I like him, and later I buy a couple of his books.

They did not know
the while they planned strike
to gain a raise of fifty cents a day
and barred the mine to scabs
that it would be this way
far away
standing astride the dawn
*to bar the highway to Madrid.**

Later that evening Homer Stevens comes in, looking for the phone number of Alderman Harry Rankin, one of the union's lawyers. He has spent the morning, not terribly fruitfully, on the herring negotiations, and the afternoon answering mail, planning the *Greenpeace* demonstration, and trying to deal with some problems in an embryonic dogfish operation on which he has a meeting the next morning. The next day he will also be setting up an agenda for an upcoming meeting of gillnet fishermen, and negotiating again on herring.

We meet, finally, on Saturday, in his roomy bungalow in Port Guichon, just outside Ladner. Across the road, a dike holds back the murky tidal waters of the Fraser delta. Fifty yards away, his father still lives in the house Stevens was born in, forty-eight years ago. His father was a fisherman and small-time *entrepreneur* with a fish-collecting and retailing business. In those days, Port Guichon was largely scow-houses, shacks built on barges and towed up and down the coast to be beached wherever the work happened to be. The community was "polyglot," Stevens re-

*From *Confederation and Other Poems*, Vancouver, 1966

members: Poles and Yugoslavians, East Indians, Chinese, Japanese, Italians.

"We were the non-Anglo-Saxons," he grins. The kids from Port Guichon–"wops and dagoes and hunkies, they called us"–got thumped by the Ladner teachers and fought it out in the schoolyard, then came home and fought among themselves.

"I can remember going out here at the age of sixteen and getting into a fight with the Japanese, a really racist goddam thing. A dozen Japanese and a dozen non-Japanese, and getting into almost a war out here in the middle of the night, fighting for the opportunity to fish." After that scrap, Stevens' father, a union man, a strong co-op member and chairman of the local CCF, took young Homer aside.

"He said, 'Look, I've never got to the stage where I've told you I don't want you in the house. But don't ever come back and tell me you've been involved in one of those things again, or I don't want you in the house.'

"Well, that made me stop and think, what have I got myself into? And I had to do a real thorough re-examination. But that was strictly an economic thing, and when you suddenly wake up, you know, what the hell were you fighting over?"

In Port Guichon in the 'thirties, you soon learned the economic facts of life. One morning a fisherman uncle came in from a night of gillnetting with 500 humpback salmon, which he sold at the going rate of a cent a fish. He had a few extra.

"I got the bright idea, by Jesus, I'll take some and I'll go and sell 'em. So I took ten, and drove around on my bicycle and found farmers and other people only too happy to take a salmon at their door for ten cents. I came back, got some more, and kept doing this till I'd sold fifty. So for fifty salmon I had $5.00, and he worked all goddam night out there on the river to produce five hundred, for five bucks. Well, you learn something out of that, you know–the vast difference, the exploitation."

Stevens' own grandparents on one side came from an island on the Yugoslav-Italian border. The other set consisted of a Greek immigrant fisherman and a Songhee Indian girl from a reserve near Esquimalt. She died in 1970, just a few months short of her hundredth birthday. As a boy, Stevens spent the summers with her in the Gulf Islands. She was, he recalls with a nostalgic smile, "really quite a person.

"She could manoeuvre a canoe and spear a fish about as well as anybody that ever tried to do it, regardless of sex. She'd think nothing of taking me and a blanket, and maybe an old pot and some salt and some tea, and we'd be gone for maybe two or three days just paddling around in a cedar dugout. She'd be spearing some fish, and when a storm'd come up she'd just pull the canoe up on the beach and get in behind a big spruce tree. I'd be scared to death, you know, wind blowing and howling, trees crashing, rain coming down, and she'd say, Never mind, sonny, never mind; this is a good tree. We're all right in here."

And, on request, Stevens explains spear-fishing: the fourteen-foot double-pronged spear, the effect of refraction in the water, how you aim the spear. To this day, his idea of a good time is to get out in the Fraser marshes, camp out and bake a salmon; or, in season, hunt ducks or moose, camp with his family on a remote lakeshore. Grace Stevens is the daughter of a union fisherman too; they have three sons and a daughter. How long since Homer was a working fisherman? He shakes his head.

"Too long." He became a full-time organizer in 1946, in his twenty-third year. But by then he had already been a fisherman nearly a decade, beginning with summer work on a Fraser River gillnetter. In 1941 he quit Grade 12 to go trawling, and for the next five years he alternated between summer gillnetting and winter trawling. By 1944, at twenty-one, he was skipper of a four-man trawler fishing off the Queen Charlotte Islands and the west coast of Vancouver Island, having been rejected for pilot training by the RCAF due to a weak right eye. He was also rejected by the Navy, and in mid-war he was classified as more valuable in food production than in the service.

In the 'thirties and 'forties, B.C.'s fishermen were divided up among several small regional associations, and subdivided again according to the kind of gear the various fishermen used. Stevens joined the B.C. Fishermen's Protective Association before he was out of junior high school, but resigned to join the United Fishermen's Federal Union in 1942. Ultimately most of the small unions merged to become the United Fishermen and Allied Workers, and when the Ladner local was formed in 1943, Stevens, not yet twenty, was elected secretary, "mainly, I think, because the other members figured here was a punk who could write minutes." Within a few weeks he was a delegate to the Annual Convention, which elected him to the union's governing body, the General Executive Board. He served continuously for twenty-four years. From 1945 to 1947 he was vice-president, and from 1948 to 1969 general secretary treasurer. Since 1969 he has been president.*

"Look, the titles don't matter very much," says Ken Campbell, manager of the Fisheries Association of B.C., the companies' organization. "Homer Stevens was the power in that union when he was secretary treasurer, and when he moved to the presidency the power moved with him." Campbell describes Stevens as "tenacious, intelligent, a very effective bargainer. He's careful, well-prepared, dedicated and sincerely concerned about the welfare of his membership. He's very firm."

True, says the reticent fishing executive. "When he gives his word he keeps it. He's never reneged on a deal, and a contract with his union, once it's signed, is pretty well honoured, which isn't so with lots of unions. He's done a great deal for the fishermen. You don't have many problems with him—except at negotiating time." Dick Hanham of the Canadian Brotherhood of Railway, Transport and General Workers, one of the United Fishermen's rivals in the Maritimes, calls Stevens "a very effective trade unionist. He's shown the degree of courage that's necessary in a very difficult industry, and he's a man with few enemies on the West Coast."

But he does have enemies, and they describe him as cunning and slippery, a fellow you have to watch, a Communist who wants to disrupt the economic process and so would as soon strike as not. What about his connection with the Communist Party? "It's no secret," Stevens shrugs. "I've been a member of the Communist Party for twenty-five or twenty-six years, give or take a couple or three years that I've been in disagreement on various issues." Precisely what issues? He'd rather not talk about them: every political party has internal disagreements, and its enemies will always use them against the party. When Stevens

*He resigned and went back to fishing in 1977.

doesn't want to talk about something, he can't be pushed. He shifts the conversation slightly but crucially, or holds it to a certain level of generality. "It had to do with the rights and responsibilities of individuals within the party. I try to live by my conscience and when I felt that certain things weren't being handled properly I tendered a resignation. But at the same time I said I was going to discuss those differences further with the Communist Party." Other people say that one of the issues was the Czechoslovakian invasion.

Ken Campbell feels Stevens pushes too hard, holds on too long to relatively minor demands. "A good labour leader has to know when to quit. It's embarrassing to be repudiated by your membership when you're recommending that a company offer *not* be accepted—but that's what happened to Homer this year." Jim Bury, the representative of the Canadian Food and Allied Workers' Union who did much of the organizing which cut the United Fishermen's feet out from under them in Canso Strait, is more critical of Stevens than the companies. "The tragedy in Canso Strait," he declares, "was that there was not sufficient groundwork for that strike. It's unfair to the members to take on a fight where the odds are so strongly stacked against you." Stevens and his colleagues were "unkind and not very realistic," and the union's failure to accept its leaders' recommendation in 1971 "indicates they're fed up with long protracted strikes that don't get anything. The companies don't respect Homer's strength: that's why they can take him on in that way."

"No union, big as it might be, is a power all to itself," Stevens replies, pointing out that Bury's own union, with half a million members in its parent organization, the Chicago-based Amalgamated Meatcutters and Butcher Workmen, nevertheless was unable to enforce its picket lines in Burgeo, Newfoundland, and ultimately could do nothing about the company's closure of the plant. And the 1971 strike vote? The United Fishermen's practice, says Stevens, is to send out research material to the locals and ask them to suggest negotiating objectives. These suggestions are harmonized at a meeting of all the locals, and company offers are submitted to the membership. During the first vote this year, a small turnout voted 86 per cent to strike; the second vote brought out more members, and a drop to 75 per cent. A large turnout the third time voted 54 per cent to accept. Stevens frowns.

"It happened once before, in '57, I think. What we found was that there wasn't nearly as much participation in the earlier stages of the process as there should have been. But okay, we'd say, it's your democratic right to stay away from meetings, it's your democratic right to come in and vote the contract in even though it's not as good as it should have been, and"–he shakes his head–"it's your democratic right to work under that contract for the next two years."

Is the union sometimes bull-headed about minor issues? "That's a slightly modified form of what the Fisheries Association would say. And of course that *has* to be their pretence: that the strike is not in the interests of the fishermen and that the companies had no part in starting it."

Stevens is very clear about his relation to the companies: they are "exploiting the fishermen," which means profiting from other men's labour, a kind of Marxist Original Sin. As the labour movement has aged, it has largely been incorporated into capitalism: in return for economic concessions, union leaders deliver a docile labour force. Unionization, says the U.S. Taft-Hartley Act, "promotes the flow of commerce by removing certain recognized sources of industrial strife." Some unions, it admits, "burden" or "obstruct" commerce. "The elimination of such practices is a necessary condition of the rights" granted workers under the Act. When the workers wildcat, the union, not management, disciplines them.

"Why sure," says Stevens, "Trade unions are a product of capitalism. But they're not tied to it, and they provide a vehicle for changing it." A good organizer, he believes, should normally come from the industry, and should know it inside out; he should be able to explain things to others, to inspire in them his own conviction that they can win. He should like people and be able to bring them together. He should trust them to make their own decisions: it is "absolutely vital" that members should feel the union to be *their* organization, not something managed for them by remote professionals. And the good organizer will always put himself in the position of the men.

So Homer Stevens spends two to six weeks a year on the union's boat, *Chiquita III*, out on the fishing grounds. Like secretary treasurer Jack Nicholls and business agent Glenn McEachern, he is paid $178.00 a week–roughly what a West Coast fisherman makes. He does not hob-nob with management. With most union leaders, says Ken Campbell, you get together for a drink or a chat after the meeting, but not with Homer Stevens. "I've known him twenty years," Campbell muses, "and I still don't feel I know the guy." Yes, he agrees, Stevens is in a way an old-time unionist who fights companies and doesn't accept the rights of management.

The United Fishermen is not labour's overseer, but its voice, and thus, necessarily, a deeply political union. Stevens believes that the officers may educate and recommend, but not dictate. In 1968, a court order directed the officers to lift the picket lines in Prince Rupert. But the members had voted to set the pickets up, and the officers argued that they took orders from the members, not *vice versa*. In a referendum, the members voted to defy the order. Stevens and the union's then-president, Steve Stavenes, were cited for contempt of court. "We argued," says Stevens, that the order "was contrary to the whole idea of the right of the membership to decide." Unimpressed by such arcane theories of democracy, the court sent Stevens and Stavenes to Thurlow Mountain Prison Camp for a year.

Even in gaol, Stevens was a thorn in the side of the authorities. On July 30, 1968, B.C. Attorney-General Leslie Peterson released a statement calling Stevens "a continual agitator" and "a negative influence" in the prison camp, where he had raised questions about "food, policy, staff and other matters that caused difficulty for the maintenance of order and discipline." Prisoners are only allowed to make collect calls, and Stevens had offered to pay for another inmate's call to a New Westminster hospital where his wife had been taken. Stevens quietly points out that he hadn't had a confrontation, not wanting to make things rougher for his friend, but one can imagine the guard impaled on that glittering gaze, rationally confronted with the irrationality of the regulations he had to defend, and shrieking at last that Stevens should keep his nose out of what didn't concern him. Stevens lost fifteen days' good behaviour time. Refusing to intercede, Peterson remarked disdainfully that Stevens "apparently feels that he has to speak for all prisoners on all matters–no doubt because of his previous position as a union leader."

Where does the union go from here? Turfed out of the old Trades and Labour Congress in 1954 ostensibly for an anti-raiding editorial in *The Fisherman*–"actually that was part of the really strong attack on the left in those years, which badly weakened the political awareness and the unity of the labour movement"–the United Fishermen have been told they can get into the mainstream Canadian Labour Congress only by merger with a CLC affiliate. The Congress suggested the CFAWU, but after the Canso Strait raids it might as well have suggested mating a cat with a dog. The Canadian Brotherhood of Railway, Transport and General Workers, however, though a rival for the East Coast fishermen, supported the United Fishermen during the Canso Strike, and Stevens' Ottawa trip involved merger talks. As fishing companies merge into food conglomerates, the 6,000-odd fishermen are in a weaker position, and the 30,000 member CBRT could use the extra muscle in its marine arm.

"Something may come of it," says Stevens. "But whether it does or not, the concept of unity goes far beyond merger. We couldn't have gotten anywhere in Canso Strait without the support of thousands of brother unionists–pulp workers and construction workers and miners and steelworkers. It was Winston Ruck, the president of the Sydney Steelworkers' local, who said at a meeting in Mulgrave, 'We just can't let the fishermen lose, because if they lose, we lose.' " Unions, Stevens believes, have to get back to some real feeling of unity. Not only should unions be reaching out to one another, but to people in the community as well. Unions are people's organizations, and must draw all kinds of people together, in a common fight for social justice. "An injury to one is an injury to all, and a victory is a victory for everybody."

The Nova Scotia Family Compact, says someone who knows, really respects Homer Stevens–and really fears him. No wonder. (December, 1971)

The Publisher, the Predators and the Paranoid Parrot:

"Fuddle-duddle you," said the parrot. That isn't exactly what she said, mind you, but any student of Prime Ministerial diction will understand what is meant.

Lyn Hancock, first wife of biologist-filmmaker-publisher-flier-author and general environmental salesman David Hancock, couldn't stand the word, um, "fuddle-duddle." Scarlet, the parrot, couldn't stand Lyn, can't stand anyone who gets at all intimate with her mate David. The three were in the cab of a pickup on the Alaska Highway, and a couple of swats had convinced the reluctant Scarlet that in such closed quarters she couldn't get away with physically attacking Lyn. What's a jealous parrot to do?

A PORTRAIT OF

DAVID HANCOCK

Scarlet scuttled back and forth along the top of the truck's seat, muttering foul oaths to herself in parrot talk. And then, abruptly, she leaned over against Lyn's ear and said—well—said what it was that she said.

She said it without pause, for the next twenty miles. Eighty-seven times, in fact, trotting first over to Lyn's ear, then back to David's.

Getting close to Hancock, one soon discovers, means getting close to animals—and getting into scrapes. "Flying with Hancock," declares his longtime associate Gordon Cooper, "is a pretty hairy experience. He'll spot an eagle's nest, and down he goes, right on top of it, parks a wing-tip on the top of the tree and circles round in a tight bank, counting chicks and eggs."

Hancock started flying in high school. The day he graduated, he bought a light airplane and a movie camera.

"The thing is, I was interested in flying because I had gotten interested in falconry," Hancock reflects. "I was so wrapped up in the magnificence of these birds and the way they fly that I wanted to do the same thing, in a very primitive and barbaric way, in an airplane."

Falconry. Hunting with trained birds. I always thought of it as an ancient sport, an affair of knights and courtiers in singlets, doublets and triplets, a mediaeval pastime which stood to hunting as boiling oil and catapults stand to warfare. It certainly never occurred to me that a high school boy almost exactly my own age, living fifty miles away, might be pursuing an interest in falconry, of all things.

"I had my pilot's licence," Hancock continues, "but I had to support myself while I logged the 300 hours of flying I needed to get my commercial licence. So I bought a truck and took up a dry-cleaning route. It was almost like working for myself, picking my own hours. I could work like hell all morning and then go flying in the afternoon. That went on till I got my commercial licence, and then I went what they call 'chisel chartering.'"

For three years Hancock flew machinery parts to isolated work camps, picked up people and equipment from nooks and crannies along the B.C. coast. Beaches rim Vancouver Island, and Hancock claims to have landed on virtually every one of them. And all the while he was looking at the wildlife, particularly the birds of prey. Hawks. Falcons. Eagles.

"I really liked bush flying," he grins. "It was a lot of fun. Yet at the same time I was still being told, *You go to such-and-such a bay, and pick up so-and-so*. But if I saw some eagles hovering over the water, fishing herring or something, I wanted to hover around and watch them, or if I saw some caribou up in the mountains behind Bella Coola I wanted to stay there. And the only real future in flying was getting into an airline–TCA, or whatever–and that really becomes a bus job."

He was still training birds of prey, and his interest in wildlife was increasing. Hancock decided to go to university and study wildlife, using the flying as a tool. He did a B.Sc. at the University of Victoria, twenty miles from the family home on the Saanich Peninsula, and went on for a Master's degree at UBC. He wrote his thesis on eagles.

"I was always interested in the predator-prey relationship," he explains. "That relationship is one of the directing forces in all of nature, evolution and so on. What makes predators tick? What stimulates them to hunt? That goes back to falconry, too: in training wild birds to hunt partly at your command, every time you release the bird you're almost having a controlled experiment. It's a *unique* opportunity to observe this predator-prey relationship at close hand. The average individual or even the biologist can go out and watch nature for years on end, and he never ever sees a preregrine falcon come down closely and strike a duck, or even attempt to strike one. But you can go out as a falconer and you can have that experience six times every day."

The killer journalist in me went into a controlled dive, and struck. I mentioned Cameron's Theory of Academic Theses, which holds that a student working on a thesis only *appears* to be solving an intellectual problem; in fact he's usually engaged on a passionate search for truths about himself. In London, once, I met a black American who was writing a thesis on African history, and it flashed on me that he was exhuming the knowledge of his own ancestors which had been buried under centuries of slavery and oppression. I felt quite smug about my discovery. Then I realized that I was a Scots-descended citizen of a threatened nation, writing a thesis on the national novelist of a country which had actually been absorbed into its rich, powerful southern neighbour. Studying Sir Walter Scott and Scotland, I was learning a good deal about Cameron and Canada.

"Do you mean," asks Hancock, "that *I'm* a predator?"

I don't know. Are you?

"Well...could be, I suppose." Introspection makes Hancock nervous; he squirms and coughs and makes jokes. I asked what makes David Hancock run: he replied that he ran from angry men bigger than himself, he ran to get out of the rain. I asked about his apparent inability to harness himself into working for someone else: he giggled a bit, and said that he thought that to run your own life your own way was one of life's finest challenges.

To get out and find eagles, Hancock used his plane. "It was absolutely indispensable," he declares. "Without it my thesis would have been completely impossible." He also found an Australian girl working in a Vancouver coffee shop, ready to embark for home after four years of wandering. Instead she spent a weekend roaring over the treetops of Vancouver Island counting eagles and entertaining a proposal of marriage. Within a month they had flown to Perth, Australia, married and returned, birdwatching all the way. Within two months Lyn Hancock was housemother to a fur seal named Sam. For a full description of actually being *married* to Hancock, consult Lyn's book, *There's A Seal in my Sleeping Bag.* By the end of the book the Hancock household includes Sam; a gibbon; a bear cub; three cougar kittens; two coatimundis; a porcupine; a Canada goose; and divers ducks, eagles, falcons and seabirds. And Scarlet, the parrot.

"I had always envisioned parrots as miserable, nasty birds who were in little cages and couldn't fly," Hancock explains, "bad dispositions, cranky—*bleagh*! But once when we were in a eucalyptus forest in Australia I heard this incredible, raucous noise off in the distance, maybe a mile and a half away, coming closer and closer—and then suddenly—flying *through* the trees, not *over* them but among the branches, came this whole flock of red-and-black cockatoos, flying *fast*, like bloody falcons, yelling and screaming."

Hancock's hands are zooming and soaring, banking and gliding; his face is alight with pleasure.

"*Zhungg! Zhungg!* through the branches, and then they'd shoot up through the tree canopy and come diving down again, yelling and screeching–*well*! I fell in love with the bloody things! I always liked things that could fly *well*. They weren't nasty creatures that couldn't fly, they could fly magnificently!

"I got back here, and a zookeeper said, would you like this miserable nasty parrot that's been stuck in this cage and can't even fly? They'd had her twenty-five years, the last six in a backroom cage, and she'd become so miserable nobody could even get into her cage to clean it out. They told me she'd been given to the zoo by a little old lady who'd had her all her life. She's a South American macaw, actually, from the Brazilian jungle. Probably about sixty now, quite an old parrot.

"Well, I looked at her, and she had broken tailfeathers and– oh, God. But I said all right, and brought her home.

"We had a big steel cage outside, a cougar cage, and we put her in there. Oh, she was a miserable, nasty bird all right. I went out towards her with my big heavy falconry gloves on, and every time you went near her she'd reach out with that great big beak of hers and try to tear you apart. This went on for three or four days.

"So I tried another tack. I went out to her this particular day, and she reached out and bit me–and I yelled *No!*–and I clobbered her, hit her broadside with my hand. I went down towards her and offered her my hand, and she bit it again. So I yelled *No!* again, and I clobbered her again; she went a good distance across the room. I walked over a third time, put my glove down, and she cocked her head and looked at me, and then reached out and grabbed it again, quickly. So I shouted *No!* and belted her again.

"But the next time I offered her my hand she looked up at me, ruffled her feathers up sideways, and stepped up on the glove. I reached over with my bare hand, and stroked her. And since then she and I have been in love. She'll let me do anything I want with her, I can take her and hold her upside down, we have big war games, we both yell and I pull her feathers, and she just loves it."

Scarlet does actually take David to be her mate, going into her mating position when he comes to her cage, trying to entice him into her nest. David has exercised her neglected wings and given her flying lessons. Though she still can't take off without being launched, she's capable of a few circuits over the house, and she sometimes delights him by landing on his arm. But she's bitterly jealous of anyone who's around David on a steady basis. Casual visitors she treats politely–but once they become regulars they're in trouble. She hated Lyn; after Lyn and David were divorced and David re-married, she quickly learned to hate Susan Im Baumgarten, his second wife, equally cordially.

We all know parrots don't actually understand what they're saying, but Scarlet has come up with some surprisingly apt remarks. Nobody knows, for instance, where she learned to curse like a Prime Minister, nor how she realized that would be a perfect weapon to use in a truck on the Alaska Highway. Another time David and Lyn were sitting together on a chesterfield. Scarlet was on his lap, watching for a chance to reach over and nip Lyn. Suddenly she made her move, and Lyn swatted her with a rolled-up magazine.

"Stop that!" Scarlet yelled, falling onto the floor. She took another nip at Lyn's ankle, and Lyn swatted her again. Lying on her back on the floor, fending off the magazine with her feet and trying to twist herself around for another snap at Lyn, she burst out with, "Stop that! I'm a bird! Stop that! I'm a bird!" She had never said anything of the kind before.

"Once you get interested in birds of prey, or any other creature, you become concerned for the animal itself, and this is the evolution of conservation," says Hancock. "Once you enjoy something and appreciate it, then you want to see it conserved and preserved." Even before going to university, Hancock knew he wanted to do something to make people aware of the fecundity and richness of Canada's declining wildlife, particularly the wildlife of the Pacific coast. His safaris in search of eagles and falcons drew the attention of the newspapers; disgusted with their failures to understand what he was really about, Hancock began taking photographs and writing articles for national magazines himself.

Vancouver television producer Bob Fortune saw some of the

articles, and suggested to Hancock that he get a movie camera and do some films for television. To Fortune's surprise, Hancock replied that he had had his own movie camera ever since high school, but he had never been able to afford film for it. Fortune overcame *that* particular obstacle, and the Hancocks made a series of fourteen half-hour shows.

That experience in turn led Hancock to the idea of feature films, flogging the environmental message in the guise of entertainment. In Canada, however, the problem with films is distribution; most movie theatres are foreign-owned and bring in the big box-office films from Hollywood rather than messing about with untested Canadian ventures. Hancock came up with a typically gung-ho solution: distribute the films himself.

They made a film called *Coast Safari*, filming during the summer, editing during the fall, and hitting the road with it during the winter. Gordon Cooper acted as advance man, going into a town, booking a hall, running ads in the local paper. The day of the showing he and Hancock would plaster all the cars downtown with handbills. The film had no soundtrack; Hancock narrated it live. Afterwards he would answer questions. Next day they would push on.

"We never made anything," Hancock reflects, "But we got our money back, and that was enough to finance the next tour." The second film, *Pacific Wilderness*, was promoted and distributed the same way. They kept at it for "seven or eight years—and it raised havoc in my life all around. You see, you've got to keep showing the film *every night*, every night that film isn't shown you lose money. I'd be away for five months every summer, filming, which was great, and then I'd be away for five months lecturing with it, *had* to be; that was the only time I was getting any revenue from the whole thing."

The way out appeared almost accidentally, if a shrewd sense of opportunity can be considered an accident.

"After we'd been touring with the films for a couple of years," Hancock explains, "we discovered that the kind of people who were coming wanted a little bit more information, and why not a book? So, just prior to going off on a summer's expedition one year, we assembled a bunch of the magazine articles and bound them together in a book called *Wild Islands*. And then I'd done so many articles on eagles alone that we bound a bunch of these together into a little booklet on the eagles themselves. We intended them strictly for sale at the film showings, you see?

"Now a lot of our film promotion was done through television. We'd go on television and talk about the film, where and when it was to be shown; and we got good television coverage, because we had good visuals in the wildlife footage. As it turned out, I took the books along and showed them on television, and the very first time I did that, before I got out of the television station three bookstores phoned up and said, 'Hey, how can we get copies of that? If you're going to be talking about a book like that, we want to sell it.'

"So we found ourselves in the book business, and with Gordon and I touring all over with the films we developed a very good distribution system around B.C. and the whole northwest. Then we took on a couple of other books for another person, and we wound up selling more of his books out in the little towns than he was selling in the cities, where he was handling them himself. So he said, 'Why don't you publish my next one?' and we did."

By 1973 the publishing business was going well enough to become a full-time operation operating out of a collection of ex-army huts on the beach near Sidney. Cooper developed his own business as a publisher's representative, handling several other lines as well as Hancock's. Hancock House put out seven books that year and fourteen in 1975. The house specializes in West Coast subjects, especially natural history and Indians; its books provide, says Hancock, fairly authoritative information for the advanced layman.

Hancock, I think, is one of those strangely compelling birds of prey one might call the Vibrant Right-Wing Charmer, hatched in the same nest as John Bassett and Enoch Powell. Such men vibrate with energy, which seems to derive from their force of will, their calm assumption that the world will just naturally make way for them. They are often libertarians, but their libertarianism is economic as well as personal, and often encompasses corporations.

Hancock's quaint faith in the free market, for instance, is based on his absolute confidence in his own ability to compete. He is upset, he declared early one morning as Gordon Cooper and I chewed our bacon on the ferry to Vancouver, about the small literary presses.

"There's no *check* on them," he frowned. "They don't have to make money; in fact some of them don't give a damn about whether their books are sold or not. They get their grant and publish the book, and if it's never sold who cares? They don't *have* to meet the test of the marketplace. A lot of what they produce is just garbage anyway, and if people won't buy it, why should it be subsidized?"

I muttered something about the dangers of monitoring the editorial policies of small presses, and something about the viability of poetry, about Al Purdy and Irving Layton, John Newlove and George Bowering, all the good poets who started in mimeograph.

"That's fine!" cried Hancock. "Fine! And I'm glad there are people around who want to publish them. But why should we *subsidize* their hobby any more than we subsidize snowmobiling?"

In Nova Scotia, I grinned, the provincial government does nothing much for writers and publishers, but it *does* offer grants to snowmobile clubs. Hancock snorted something about everyone having their hands in the public pocket, then jumped from his chair.

"Lot of wildlife around here," he explained, "eagles, and–look–there's that colony of Steller sea lions." The ferry was virtually scraping the banks of Active Pass. "Twelve, fourteen–you usually see more than that." I peered, then caught them: a dozen heads in the water off a rocky spit, looking like wet black balloons.

"You've been at the Writers' Union, eh?" said Hancock, putting sucaryl in his coffee. "Now that's the silliest damn thing I ever heard of. What on earth does a writer want with a union?"

"Same thing as a plumber," I said. "A fair wage."

"Aaaagh!" grunted Hancock.

"No, look," I explained, "I had a call from an editor in Toronto the other day. He's looking for a book review. To read the book and write the review is two days' work, and he says the best he can offer me is $25.00."

"So don't *do* it!" Hancock cried.

"No, but the point is his attitude: he's got money to spend on the long distance phone, and you can bet he doesn't try his sob story on Ma Bell at the end of the month. He doesn't try it on the landlord, or Ontario Hydro, or the printer or the distributor. But he'll try it on a writer."

"Look," said Hancock, "It's very simple. You're a professional, you're worth good money, and either he pays what you're worth or he gets someone else. Nobody's forcing you to write for him. You don't need any union. That standard contract the union is after, now, there's no way I'd sign that. Absolutely no way! No publisher would."

"McClelland and Stewart did," I said.

"They did? They *did*?"

"Yeah, with a novelist in the union."

"Well, maybe with a novelist it's different," Hancock shrugged. "But the kind of publishing I do, there's no way I'd sign it. It's totally unrealistic. This business of assigning the Canadian publisher only the Canadian rights..."

It went on like that. We were still at it going down the companionway to the car deck. Hancock's associates are convinced he would close the firm down rather than deal with a union in his own business. A charming bird of prey, I tell you.

We drove off the ferry, up the freeway to Vancouver, Cooper's truck swaying under its load of books. Hancock's little orange Mazda station wagon pulled up beside us, rolled down its window.

"Gordon!" shouted Hancock. "Will you pick up seventy-five copies of *Koona* in Vancouver for me?"

"All right," Cooper called.

The two vehicles swerved apart, Hancock holding his wheel with one hand as he leaned across the front seat. He swung back beside us.

"And tell Cameron," he yelled, "that I've thought of *another* reason why he's only *worth* twenty-five bucks!"

(April 6, 1975)

59

Philosopher of Liberty:

The radio crackles out the news from B.C.: Bennett the Younger, after acting for several years like a management consultant, has revealed the old Social Credit fanaticism. His government will institute compulsory treatment for drug addicts, "in preparation for a drug-free society."

Thank God for Donald Brown, a reliable sea anchor against the high winds now blowing from the far right.

Donald Brown is a philosopher who believes that such musty old mannequins as Aristotle, Descartes and John Stuart Mill still have something useful to say about the issues which perturb us now. For Brown, philosophy is not an abstruse, scholastic affair, pursued by bookish eccentrics in ivied towers; philosophy is a

A PORTRAIT OF

DONALD BROWN

process of thinking hard about the most difficult and important questions there are. What is the nature of life? What is the good, or the beautiful? What is knowledge?

Unlike most intellectuals, Brown worries a good deal about whether his thinking is "faithful to reality," and he takes his citizenship seriously. The result has been a series of provocative statements bringing philosophy to bear on such matters as abortion, the rights of children, euthanasia, and drugs. Brown can reply to Bennett's proposals for compulsory treatment on a moment's notice: he has already published his opinion in a brilliant 1972 paper in the *UBC Law Review*, under the cheeky title "Drugs and the Problem of Law Abuse."

"A robust sense of the issues must surely put first a simple point, which can be crudely stated as follows," Brown wrote. "Compulsory treatment is nonsense, because there is no treatment. Subjection to it is then worse than nonsense, it is injustice.

"I share John Stuart Mill's gut indignation at the abuse of power and the insolence of office," Brown grins, leaning back in his chair in his spartan third-floor office in the University of British Columbia's Buchanan Building. "And it has always seemed to me natural and proper that one's academic work should be continuous with one's interests as a citizen, or just as a person."

When I enrolled in his second-year Logic course in 1956, Brown was twenty-nine, newly returned from Oxford, where he had won a D.Phil. and taught for four years. He was wraith-like and tweedy, and he wore a swirling academic gown. He drove a 1938 Dodge, and though he thought faculty salaries too low, he obviously felt privileged just to be able to do philosophy for a living.

Now he is fifty, author of philosophical treatises, a distinguished full professor with a newish Dodge, and he thinks faculty salaries too high. Sporting a turtleneck and modishly long hair, he is somewhat embarrassed that I remember his gown. But he still gives the impression that it never seriously occurred to him that the good life could be anything *but* the contemplation and application of philosophical ideas.

In which belief he may well be right: after all, if one has no notion of what goodness is, how is one to make even the most ordinary of moral choices? Without some idea of a good society, how are we to cast our votes intelligently? Not content with giving his own students the greatest possible freedom of choice, Brown teamed up with several kindred spirits on and off the UBC faculty to establish Vancouver's first libertarian school, The New School, which both his children attended. In the early 'sixties he was one of the founders of the B.C. Civil Liberties Association.

"Civil liberties are perhaps a luxury," Brown remarks, citing Brecht's adage: "grub first, then ethics." And he is struck by the paradoxes of his own position. "My life has been characterized by such exceptional good luck as almost to deprive me of useful experiences," he explains. "I find myself being indignant on behalf of the underdog while not being one myself. In fact, I can hardly imagine a more secure and comfortable situation than mine in the whole society—a tenured member of a university faculty. How could you pick anything more optimally calculated to make you feel complacent and satisfied?"

But in fact civil libertarians are often secure and self-confident. Their own sense of being quite capable of directing their own lives with only minimal interference may even be one of the roots of their outlook, since what they insist on for others is exactly the same degree of liberty they demand for themselves. They feel attacks on liberty as attacks on *their* liberty. Brown often remarks on "gut reactions" and "things which get the adrenalin going."

"For example, these guys who just won their case about solitary confinement being cruel and unusual punishment—that gives me such a *jet* of pleasure: God, isn't that *nice*! Wonder who that judge is, I'd like to send him a bottle of champagne!"

Adrenalin may seem a strange stimulus for philosophical statements, but Brown's paper on the rights of children provides an example.

"That was a curious coincidence," he explains. "I happened to become very angry at the administrative act of a school principal, which seemed to me to affect freedom of speech and indeed the editorial freedom of my son"—he laughs—"and in that mood of anger I was suddenly asked by the philosophy of education people here at UBC whether I would talk about the rights of children, on which they happened to be having a conference.

"The rights of children provide one of the great test cases for Mill's theory of liberty, too; he sets up a view of liberty which is fundamentally designed for mature adults in their right minds, and the theory is in constant embarrassment on its borderlines, with respect to children, the insane, the senile, the feeble-minded, animals—and, in the future, I would think, computers and robots. There are many creatures with whom we have moral relations, but who are not full-blown moral agents, and thus present us with special problems.

"Children, of course, are a category we all deal with all the time, and we are in great confusion of mind over when a child becomes an adult, with adult rights and responsibillities. That confusion shows up at all levels—school discipline, handling of juvenile offenders, and so on." Brown argued that children have all the adult rights they are competent to exercise, and that they acquire additional rights as they acquire additional competence.

What are the basic principles from which Brown works on an issue like this?

"Well, Mill took a fairly common sense principle and embedded it in a respectable theory," Brown muses. "That's the principle that an individual may do as he pleases, within the limits of not harming other people. Now a principle like that—together with the things you need to say about how to apply it, and when it fits in, and so on—is just about adequate.

"But I want to shift the ground a bit to another principle, which is also in Mill, and which he thought came to the same thing, but it doesn't. He also said that society may interfere to enforce morality. Now that's actually a very important extension of the idea. Among the moral wrongs one may do is not only harming people, but failing to help them when you have an obligation to do so. And that's part of the basis of the welfare state: that the state coerces people to help people who are unable to help themselves.

"Now that is what I think morality *is*. Very roughly, not harming people, and helping them when you have to, is not a bad summary of the content of morality. Within those broad bounda-

63

ries, one may claim the right to do whatever he thinks fit."

And so we find Brown, in a piece written for the op-ed page of the Vancouver *Sun*, arguing that the right to dispose of one's life as one sees fit must include the right to voluntary euthanasia, or a form of "assisted suicide" for "those who are fatally ill, and want to die with dignity or without pain." Unlike some other would-be suicides, "they are people for whom suicide is a rational decision, and we must ask ourselves whether, as a society, we respect their position." Evidently we don't: a person fatally ill may be unable to kill himself without help and the Criminal Code provides stiff penalties for anyone who helps him.

What are some other current civil liberties issues? Brown thinks for a moment, then mentions penal reform, the proper use of personal information, and abortion.

Abortion is the subject of a 1972 position paper Brown wrote for the B.C. Civil Liberties Association. "There is nothing to be said for abridging rights important to women, or for having any criminal restriction on abortion, except the claim that an embryo or fetus has some right to protection," he wrote. But "if we obliterate the difference between embryos and fetuses, on the one hand, and persons on the other, and if we attempt to extend to the former the principles which apply to the moral relations among persons, we violate common sense. After an abortion, as after a miscarriage, it seems merely reasonable to deny that there exists or ever has existed any person who has died or been killed. Both in morality and in law, all the obligations we owe are owed to actual persons and not to merely possible persons."

Admitting that many people have a sincere moral objection to abortion, Brown insisted that "both sides should recognize that the disagreement makes it desirable for the law to be silent, and to leave decisions about abortion to the conscience of the individuals concerned. It is a matter of conscience on both sides, since many people believe there are occasions on which it is a moral duty to have an abortion. Those who have a moral or religious objection to abortion are of course left free to act accordingly."

Brown considers himself a "liberal," a description hardly anyone nowadays aspires to.

"I resent the way the word has been trampled on and become dirty, sure," Brown admits. "Mind you, the liberal tradition has sins to be atoned, in that believing in principles of liberty has gone with callousness towards social justice and inequality, so that I can understand how blacks in the States—and many others—become bitter about liberals whose liberalism is for themselves, and for their kind, and not for everybody. But conceived as a moral view of the relations between society and the individual, liberalism seems to me something which is not to be given up, and which even Marxists can embrace."

To my mind, the finest application of Brown's principled liberalism to a concrete social issue remains his 1972 article on drugs and the law, a paper which not only offers a scathing critique of our present narcotics law, but also suggests a whole alternative approach, and provides an admirable example of the kind of intellectual leadership the university community generally prefers to shirk.

"One conclusion that I think clearly emerges from applying liberal principles to the law," Brown declares, "is that the possession of a drug ought not to be an offence. I mean *any* drug — heroin, speed, barbiturates, grass of course. Simple possession or use of a drug is not, in itself, conduct harmful to anybody else, so that if you want to argue it on the grounds of legal principles, you can say that possession laws, as such, are standing invasions of civil liberties. But this corresponds very exactly to the simple humanitarian remark that the heroin addict is not essentially the criminal involved, but the person on whose behalf the whole apparatus of law enforcement is justified. The humanitarian and civil liberties approaches, you see, arrive at exactly the same point."

The real victim of drug use is, if anyone, the user himself, and he "has a right to damage himself if he chooses to do so." If you don't concede him that right, how are you going to justify allowing a person to smoke tobacco, take sudden exercise, drive a car or drop out of school, any of which may have disastrous consequences and may make him a charge on public funds? If we don't want people *driving* when they're stoned, let's say, because they are likely to harm others, we can pass laws against that, as we have for alcohol. But merely getting stoned—on dope or booze—is a private decision.

"Now the trafficker certainly does some harm, to various kinds of people," Brown continues, in that gentle, firm and somehow relentless voice, "and certainly many traffickers shape up as pretty odious characters personally. But the police have pretty much admitted that they can't stop trafficking, and one reason clearly is that they lack the usual complaints from the victims, because the trafficker is essentially supplying a service and carrying the risks of an illegal business. The addict's main complaint—and, I sometimes think, the main moral objection to trafficking—is that it's economically extortionate. The pusher has a group of people at his mercy, and he exploits them economically. But as far as causing damage is concerned, it's fair to compare consumer finance companies, slum landlords and munitions manufacturers. So although trafficking is certainly a dirty business, it's no dirtier than many other businesses that are legal."

But doesn't the trafficker recruit people to become addicts? Yes, says Brown, but addiction isn't something the pusher inflicts on the user without his consent; even heroin addiction "requires the co-operation of the user through a series of choices." Okay, but the pusher surely takes advantage of the potential addict's desperate personal difficulties. Brown admits this, too. But, he writes, "consider the difference between a pusher who supplies heroin to a person unable to cope with his problems and a man who takes his depressed workmate along to get smashed on a Saturday night or a doctor who prescribes pills for a housewife who is feeling desperate. We can measure the distances as we like; we still have to admit that the three are on a continuum. It looks to me as if our indignation discharges on the pusher because we are baffled as to whom to blame for the wretchedness of the addict."

The trafficker, in Brown's view, is largely a creation of the law in the first place. "We provide a guaranteed market and an enormous profit margin. Users who crave drugs and cannot get them clinically can be counted on to buy. The drugs themselves are cheap to produce, and reward accrues to sheer enterprise and criminality at many thousand per cent. Moreover, given the perennial willingness of business to supply bombers, tobacco, alcohol and napalm, there can be no mystery in the irrepressible vitality of the drug trade. How is it then that we go on staring at these economic realities like a cow at a new gate?''

The unquestionable misery of the addict is also largely produced by the law. "We make the possessor, i.e., the user, a criminal. But we also deny him legal access even to medically supervised supply, and thereby drive him to engage in secondary crime, to deal with criminals, and to join their world. But now he really is a criminal by any standard, and so our original decision to call him a criminal has vindicated itself. We have created a situation in which becoming dependent is no longer just an unhappy situation, like being alcoholic, but a fatal plunge into a world of financial desperation, daily risk, untreated illness and despair. Our dishonesty consists in refusing to admit that this component of the misery flows from the evil in our social policy, not from the drug or the pusher."

But what *are* we to do for the addict?

"I sometimes find, echoing in my head, the old Confucian saying," Brown smiles ruefully, " *'The way out is through the door. Why is it that no one will make use of this method?'* People who take a civil liberties' line on public questions often appear in the role of nagging critics. It appears that some sensible and necessary scheme is going forward, and along comes the civil libertarian blowing the whistle and complaining that we may not do it this way because there are rules that are being broken about due process and the liberty of the individual. A civil liberties' angle is often seen as being obstructionist and tedious.

"Now I think it's generally true, and I'm *sure* it's true in the case of drugs, that the insistence on freedom and justice, in the very principled way that's characteristic of the civil libertarian, also provides the practical solution to the problem. There is certainly a serious human problem. But people are so impressed by the urgency of the problem that they have forgotten one of the most obvious options, which is simply to behave correctly towards the people involved. The 'war' on drugs has escalated through so many stages that people have forgotten just how drastic and brutal our methods have already become. They find it difficult to see that an entirely new approach can be found just by stepping back and respecting individuals."

All right, what *is* this new approach?

It begins, says Brown, by restoring the user to full citizenship, which means abolishing the offence of possession. Trafficking should be re-defined as the sale of drugs on a large scale, for profit; "no one can justify having an offence of trafficking drawn as widely as our present one, according to which handing someone a joint on a social occasion is trafficking." Trafficking should perhaps remain an offence, like bootlegging, but the goal of the police should be merely to hold the line while we address the problem through voluntary treatment—clinics, medical programs, controlled supply of drugs, counselling, group therapy, job support programs, and the like.

We should "accept any voluntarily-obtained improvement in the condition of any user as a gain, and as an acceptable interim aim of treatment." Perhaps "treatment" will mean supplying drugs to addicts indefinitely, substituting methadone for heroin, and so forth. A great deal of evidence suggests that many addicts can function perfectly well at work and otherwise, so long as their supply is assured. At the very least, the addict's desperation would be greatly eased, and he would not be driven automatically to secondary crime.

Brown is perfectly willing to admit that such a program would cost enormous amounts of money, but drug problems are costing enormous amounts already, both in secondary crime and in maintaining large narcotics squads and platoons of customs investigators. In any case, if we are not prepared to spend money to help people in need, we are a morally bankrupt society.

Such a policy, Brown claims, would also take the steam out of the drug trade. "When people have alternatives to drug use, when treatment is genuinely available, and when for those who still need them drugs are obtainable without risk, the market and the incentives will collapse together, and the vast business will have disappeared in the only way it ever will disappear, by economic evaporation."

I admire Brown's approach to the whole thorny question: I wonder whether it can ever succeed. It deprives us of scapegoats, and it lacks the dramatic power of our present holy war against the drug menace. The old morality play disappears, the upright and uptight *versus* the dope fiends and the fiendish pushers. What remains is only a group of people working steadily and unspectacularly to reduce human distress. But when we are still hearing fairyland fantasies from government about a future "drug-free society," what chance do such modest objectives stand?

All the same, it is good to have people like Brown around, actively and persistently thinking about better answers to large questions. People die from philosophical errors: the Indians of Grassy Narrows and the miners of St. Lawrence, Newfoundland, are dying now from our misconception of humanity's relation to nature and to people.

"When we were talking earlier about current issues in civil liberties," Brown remarks, "I didn't mention women's lib, which I take very seriously, and which is full of serious practical issues." Indeed it is, and before long it leads us into a discussion of marriage. Brown has been happily married for many years, and has two children; his wife Julia is a teacher and a writer of fiction. But like everyone else, Brown is puzzled and saddened by the pain of people all around him, whose marriages are shattering like glass. What *is* the nature of marriage, anyway? It's the kind of topic Brown likes to think about.

"One is tempted to regard it as a contract," he muses, "but if it's a contract, what are the terms? Nobody knows. You only find out when you're being divorced. Now one wouldn't enter into a contract in which the terms were unspecified, so it must be the case that we don't generally regard it as a contract.

"I've been reading a book by an American philosopher, David Lewis, called *Convention*, and I think it may be useful here. Lewis points out that we have all kinds of rules and expectations–conventions–which are never articulated, but which we all understand and use."

Such as?

"Well, suppose you and I are talking on the telephone, and we're cut off. Who calls the operator and re-establishes the connection?"

I think for a moment.

69

"The person who originally placed the call."

"Exactly. You see, there's a perfect convention. If both called, or neither, it wouldn't work. So there's an understanding, and each party understands that the other understands that both understand, and so on forever. Now perhaps that's a reasonable account of marriage, that it's an institution built up of a vast number of small and not-so-small conventions, and that whatever gave rise to the conventions no longer sustains them. And of course, if we don't agree on its constituent conventions, the institution itself becomes shaky."

But what *are* the conventions of marriage?

"Probably there are literally hundreds. But again, an example: it seems to me that it used to be one of the conventions of marriage that both husband and wife understood—and understood each other to understand—that their residence would be determined by the husband's occupation. I don't think that is any longer a reliable convention in marriage, and there are people among whom it is a convention of their marriage that that shall *not* be the case. On this point, there are presently two conventions about. Now when conventions are altering in that way, in a lot of different directions, then the institution itself becomes confusing to people."

Brown's own life and marriage are shifting and altering as the years go by. Now that the children are almost adults, they have sold the roomy house in West Point Grey and moved into a brand new apartment on the top of a four-storey wooden building in the West End—"lively architecture" says Brown, "cedar siding, a block shaded with catalpa trees, and right in the thick of the city." They were tired of the upkeep on the big house, and they're deep in the project of building a retreat on De Courcy Island, near Nanaimo. Eventually he foresees a life divided between the city and the university on the one side, and the retirement of the island on the other. One of the objectives is to find more time to write.

"You know," he grins, "that's really my idea of recreation: some swimming, cutting some wood, and a lot of writing."

About what? A book on Mill, which comes from his civil liberties work. And then?

"I suppose the centre of my interests all along has been the notion of what human rationality is, and in particular what rational conduct is, which overlaps with the study of ethics on the one hand, and on the other with the study of action and motivation and the structure of reasoning. There are still any number of interesting problems on which lots of people are making interesting progress these days. I think of philosophy as a communal and cumulative affair."

Does he agree that philosophy stands right at the core of human life and our attempts to understand it? To me, philosophy is *the* central intellectual discipline.

"Well, yes, partly by default," Brown nods, reminding me that philosophy has always tended to spin off other disciplines. In Aristotle's day, most of what we now call "science" was part of philosophy; more recently, psychology and linguistics have left the philosophical homestead, setting off on what Brown calls "the sure path of a science." Such fields are no longer speculative; now they are subject to precise investigation by scientific experimentation.

Philosophy, Brown explains, is more or less whatever is left. "Anything about which it's still appropriate to speculate and to reason, in a persistent and determined way—and which has not yet become a science—is by definition philosophy. So it's *bound* to be the centre, so to speak."

He pauses for a moment, and then his face breaks into that open, boyish, almost innocent grin.

"Philosophy," he announces, "is whatever's still a mess."

God bless the mess.

(January, 1974: August, 1977)

The Multiple Passions of the Natural Rebel:

Bruno Gerussi, aged perhaps fifteen, picked up his kid brother by the front of the shirt and shook him as a terrier shakes a rat.

"You're a *little wop dago!*" shouted Bruno. "Don't you forget that, you're a *little wop dago!*"

"Don't call me that!" cried Dino. "Bruno, put me down!"

"You don't like that, you little wop?"

"No!"

"All right, don't you ever let me hear you talking about 'the Japs' again, you hear? *Never.*"

Bruno Gerussi, aged forty-six, doesn't laugh when he tells that story. These days, Bruno Gerussi is Canada's ranking male TV star, a trained Shakespearean actor, an enormously successful ra-

A PORTRAIT OF

BRUNO GERUSSI

dio and TV host, a vigorous and engaging man whose friends include premiers and international celebrities. There's a quadrophonic sound system in the new BMW sedan in the driveway; inside the house another quad' system sends its music out over shag carpets and mod furniture, reverberates off the knotty cedar walls and the huge sheets of glass which command the view from Gibson's Landing up the smoky green mountains along Howe Sound. There's another house in Toronto, and a cottage in rural Ontario and—well—the Italian kid from New Westminster, B.C., is doing all right.

But he hasn't forgotten what it was like to be eleven years old when World War II broke out, and all the kids he had thought were his friends began throwing stones at him and beating him up and telling him he was a dirty wop because the Italians, you see, were on the other side. He hasn't forgotten that his mother was shipped from one end of Italy to the other in a cattle car, and that very few of her fifteen brothers and sisters have survived the horrors of modern history. He remembers his father, "an extraordinary man, really a Renaissance man," and he believes he understands what drove his father to suicide.

"I'm an optimist," Gerussi insists. "I'm a realist too; I don't go around saying, *Ohhh, the world is just sooo beautiful*; I know what a shitpit it is. But I do believe that the human being is an extraordinary piece of work, and can do anything."

He's perched on a chair in front of the huge windows, talking intensely, that famous face moving as ceaselessly as sunlight and shadow over the water, an unlit cigarette dangling from a corner of his mouth, the moustache lifting, the brows pulling together, leaning into the conversation, his hands flying—

"I don't just take my money and go away, that's not what it's all about," he frowns, snatching up a matchbook, tearing off a match. "I'm an *artist*: that's a big responsibility, and I *accept* that responsibility." He throws his hand in the air, and the matchbook shoots up out of it, glancing off the window. Gerussi catches it, strikes his match, lights his cigarette, never pausing in the conversation. "I happen to have a great deal of energy, mental and physical, and I want to use it. It's possible to do something meaningful in television, something that will be an educational force in the community."

Wait a minute, now, Bruno: we're talking about *The Beachcombers*, remember. I realize it's one of the CBC's most popular shows ever, and I admit I haven't seen a great many episodes. But the ones I *have* seen fell somewhat short of—

"Oh, sure! We've relied far too much on physical action, boats flying through the air and that kind of nonsense, and that's really meaningless; after a while it gets stale and boring. Action isn't just physical action; what goes on between characters is action too. And it's hard to keep your eye on what you're supposed to be doing when you're turning them out the way we have to, one episode every five days of shooting. All that's true, but the best of *The Beachcombers* have been bloody good, *bloody* good, and we've really built our audience.

"I was on the ferry last week and a logger came up to me, he lives up here somewhere, and he'd seen 'The Sea Is Our Friend,' an episode in which I'm trapped under a log and the tide is rising, and Jesse and Hugh have to get me out. Now this guy's a logger, he really knows what that would be like, and he told me he was up on the back of the chesterfield, right?"—jumping up, Gerussi mimes it—"with his bottle of beer in his hand *shouting* at the television set, *Come on, you guys, get that son of a bitch out! Get that son of a bitch out!!*

"Not too long ago I was up in Kitimat and I was signing autographs for five hours straight—*five hours*! You see? We *do* have the audience. I'm personally well-known, I have a certain sexual appeal—I mean this is fact, it's been written about, it's not just my idea—okay, so now we have to use that to do something meaningful."

He glances at his watch.

"Come on, let's go down to the Reach. I said I'd be there by 1.00."

"The Reach" is Molly's Reach, a cafe at the head of the government wharf around which the actions of *The Beachcombers* revolve; it was once the government liquor store. Gerussi swings the BMW into its reserved spot, sprints through the rain to the building, hustles up to the tiny offices and dressing rooms on the second floor, greeting people as he goes.

74

"Hey Bruno!" calls Elie Savoie, the producer of the series, from his cubbyhole office. "You know we nearly lost the Reach last night?"

"G'wan."

"No, seriously. A little fire broke out downstairs, but someone spotted it and turned in the alarm before it took hold."

"Jesus!" says Gerussi, shaking his head. "That's all we need."

Make-up girls with pouches of cosmetics. Hairdressers. Costume people. Gerussi's dressing room can't be more than eight feet square.

A series has its hazards. "Guys do go bananas working on series, ending up in the giggleworks or shooting themselves," Gerussi muses, pulling off his sandals and white linen trousers. In one episode, he had to give a boat the signal to pull a cable taut; the tide had moved the boat, and when the cable straightened it was only inches behind his head. "That thing can snap off trees," Gerussi shudders. "It was instant death if it had hit me. I just walked away and sat down for ten minutes and nobody said very much." Off comes the white embroidered pullover shirt and the gold nugget, suspended from a thong, which bounces on his hairy chest.

Another time the script called for a plane to skim above the water toward Gerussi's boat, pulling up just in time to clear it. The effect was easy enough with a telephoto lens, but the pilot actually came within three feet, and not just once, but six times. "All the crew was ducking down," snaps Gerussi, "but they were shooting *me*. What was I going to do? Jump overboard? I can't even swim! He's an excellent pilot and I trust him implicitly; but the *least* little slip, man! At the end of it I was just gibbering and shaking."

On goes the working garb of Nick Adonidas, independent log salvage operator and general headman of Molly's Reach.

"I don't want the mauve shirt," Bruno calls, "I want the blue, give me one of those blue work shirts. That's good. Got a pair of socks? Sure, those'll do." He sits on a couch, faces a mirror, daubs his face with make-up.

"I tan very easily," he explains, "but I lose it very easily too. I don't have to use make-up during the middle of the summer, but it's been dark and wet the last couple of weeks." He pulls an eyelid down, works the colour into the folds of the skin. When he finished high school he apprenticed with a Seattle theatre school and repertory company, studying voice and movement, building props, working the lights, even selling tickets as well as acting. That's where he learned make-up. My eye falls on a letter serving as a bookmark: dated from Clearwater, B.C., it begins, *Dear Mr. Gerussi, Our three-year-old daughter who has developed a very large crush on you. . .*

Downstairs, out into the drizzle under the lowering skies. It's too dark, even in the early afternoon, to shoot by natural light, and the crew has floodlights at the ready. A bus chartered for this particular scene stands idling at the curb. Cameramen and sound men huddle over their Nagras and Arriflexes, keeping them dry. Bubbles of brightly coloured umbrellas defy the grey sky.

At a park bench, Gus Calhoun, the bad little boy of the series, is baiting an old punch-drunk prizefighter. Margaret, Nick's ten-year-old buddy, watches Nick try to mitigate Gus' cruelty, then races off to greet her pen pal, who is arriving on the bus.

"Let's run through it," someone says, and Bruno emerges from his brolly, goes through the action. The angles aren't quite right, the scene doesn't move properly. Everyone goes into a huddle like a football team, working out the necessary changes. Another run-through. Then a take with the cameras, and another. It finally comes right: only a few lines, perhaps thirty seconds on your TV screen, but it's taken up a good chunk of the afternoon.

Bruno isn't in the next shot, and he vanishes. He reappears at the Reach with a couple of beef sandwiches, which we wolf down while we wait for his next scene. He talks aimlessly with Rae Brown, who plays Molly in the series. Bruno wants to revisit the Maritimes. He spent a summer acting at the Fredericton Play-house, and he was down once or twice with *Gerussi!*, the program of talk, music and poetry which reshaped CBC morning radio be-tween 1965 and 1971. In Prince Edward Island, he has heard, a church which serves lobster dinners in the basement during the tourist season hands out cards saying BRUNO GERUSSI ATE HERE. Gerussi laughs, but he's genuinely pleased too.

76

He's enthralled with his glimpses of Newfoundland, appalled that the Beothucks, its original Indians, were utterly exterminated by 1829 through a program of genocide most Canadians still know nothing about. Rae Brown has never heard of them, and Gerussi tells her of their ingenuity, their culture, and the savagery with which they were systematically gunned down by bounty hunters.

The troupe comes in from the rain and fog. It's only 3.30, but the light is completely hopeless; go home, everyone. Gerussi zips upstairs, returns in street clothes, and suggests we get a couple of steaks and have dinner. I protest: my notion was to take *him* out to dinner, but he overrules me. His place is a comfortable spot to talk, and there's no good restaurant nearby. Besides, he enjoys cooking.

As a matter of fact, he's hosting a cooking program next year, a daily TV show called *Celebrity Cooks*. On his days off, he flies to Ottawa, tapes a few shows, flies back. "It's a lot of fun," he declares. "We get a celebrity to talk and prepare his special dish — live — with a studio audience. It's a mixed bag, about half Canadians and half international celebrities. We're getting Barbara Hamilton, and Margaret Trudeau, Hermione Gingold, Frankie Howerd of *Up Pompeii!*, Theodore Bikel — we have a good time — and there's not too much to it so long as the guest can actually cook. Sometimes you get some guy who says Oh yeah, I got this *great* dish, and then you get to the studio and find out he's never cooked it."

At the Super Valu on the hill, Gerussi shops with the concentration of a man who really cares about his food. As he considers the cucumber, a small boy sidles up to him.

"Hey!" says the boy. "I seen you *on TV!*"

"That's right, friend. How are you?"

"Sure," says the kid, off balance, suddenly shy. "Fine, okay." He bolts. A moment later I see him come by clinging to his mother's shopping cart. "See, Mom?" he whispers. "There he *is*!"

A stop at the liquor store for wine, and we roll down the hill again, the crystal notes of Pink Floyd's *Meddle* shimmering out of the four speakers. It's a favourite of mine, and I haven't heard

77

it in the six weeks I've been away from home. I check out the other tapes on the driveshaft hump: Rita Coolidge, Vivaldi, Leon Russell's *Carney*, another favourite. I steal a glance at Gerussi, whipping joyfully along the slick, winding road, draped in linen, surrounded by leather and music. Sensual, I think: I bet he's a good cook.

Brandishing knives, shaking spices, slicing tomatoes, grilling the steaks, Gerussi throws himself into his cooking with gusto. He pours Dubonnet, slips a record on, delivers unequivocal opinions in a voice that carries from the kitchen across the living room, proudly points out the details of the yellow cedar table, admits that he himself carved the red cedar wall plaque with the Coast Indian design. His vitality tends to occupy all the space around him.

And he *is* a good cook, combining a lusty burgundy, tender steak and an astringent salad into the sort of feast that leaves one lazily burping, somnolent and satisfied. We reminisce about his radio program, to which I was an occasional contributor, and he explains how he got into radio.

One night in 1965 Ida, Gerussi's high school sweetheart and wife of fifteen years' standing, suddenly began breathing with difficulty. She died before Bruno could get her to the hospital. He was still working with the Stratford Shakespearean Festival then, and touring during the winters with the Canadian Players; he was on the verge of invading the United States with a one-man show. Finding himself a widower with two children, Gerussi left the stage for radio, which allowed him to stay in Toronto with the children.

"We all worked it out together," he remembers. "We had no maid, no housekeeper, nothing like that. We learned pretty early on that nobody owns other people, you know? They're free, and I'm free, and our connection is that we care about each other. They were out here this summer, and we had a marvellous time. Ricky, my son, is twenty-two, a very gifted musician; he's in London now, studying the guitar with an excellent teacher. I remember we were all sitting around this room—Ricky and Patsy Berton, Pierre's daughter and Tina, that's my daughter, she's eighteen and studying piano—and me and a friend, a woman I've been going out with.

"And I said, Ricky, I haven't heard you play for months; why don't you give us a song? So he got out his guitar and began to fool with it, and then these beautiful sounds began to come out of it and he started singing; it was just *marvellous*, I can't tell you how beautiful it was. When he was done, I couldn't believe it: I said, Ricky, I had no idea you'd become that good, that's professional quality. Where'd you get the song? And he said, I wrote it. Man, I was just knocked out! I think he'll probably do the caravan thing with me—I'd love that."

The caravan thing?

"Well, I won't be with *The Beachcombers* forever, though there's no reason the show can't go on forever, as long as it keeps in touch with the real concerns people have. But eventually I want to get a caravan and just go wandering across the country, giving performances in villages and church halls, you know, wherever there's an audience. I'd like to revive the old idea of the travelling minstrel, and make live performances available to people who never get to see them ordinarily.

"Prisons, for instance, I want to do shows in prisons. We have a fantastic number of people in prisons in this country, you know? Eventually we aren't going to put people in prison, we're going to put them out in the community and rehabilitate them. They're people, and we have a responsibility towards them, I firmly believe that.

"And there are some very sensitive, very intelligent people in prison. The big demand in prisons these days is for poetry, did you know that? Here, let me show you something." He thrusts his chair back, crosses to the bookcase, comes back with *Don't Steal This Book*, an anthology of writing by inmates of the Saskatchewan penitentiary. "There's some really good stuff in there, really moving. I'd like to reach people like that with a one-man show, just myself and a couple of musicians. And I want to see more of this country. I've chosen to live here, I've travelled over a great deal of it, and I feel very strongly about it."

He really likes his children.

"Yeah, I do. That's what I feel proudest of in my life–that they've turned out to be really marvellous people–they've come through all that terrible period of growing up, deciding what they want to do with themselves, coming to terms with drugs and sex and all that. They're solid, special adults now. And I helped make that possible: I *am* proud of that, of course I am."

Was he ever tempted to marry again, to provide a mother for them, for instance?

"That's the very last reason I'd ever think of marrying. They've had a mother, a wonderful rich person, and she can't be replaced. No, there was a time to be married, but not now. I'm not carrying a torch or anything, please get that clear, but I just don't think I'm willing to make those compromises any more, those compromises you have to make if you tie your life to another person in that way." He laughs. "My mother asked me that one time." He mimics an Italian accent. "*Bruno, whatsa matter you don't get married again, a young man like you?*' Ma, I said, why didn't *you*? She looked at me for a long time, and then she smiled and shrugged. *'Ah, Bruno, Bruno. You booger, you.*'"

His father was a bricklayer by trade, a self-taught musician by avocation, a creative soul with no chance to live a creative life. "He wanted to be a violinist, a concert violinist, and it was just too *late.* And that kind of frustration, not being able to live his life the way he really wanted to because of domestic obligations, financial obligations, bringing up a family–you know–eventually that kind of thing piles up. He'd go into deep depressions, and he–well–he had a nervous breakdown and had to go to hospital, mental hospital. Then he went into a kind of religious mysticism, and this went on, on and off, over a long period–you know–he'd be fine for three or four years and then bang, he'd have a spell and he'd just become totally depressed and have to go to the hospital.

"He was a trumpet player originally, cornet actually, and he taught himself to play the violin in the mental hospital, borrowed a violin from another patient and painstakingly figured out and wrote down where each and every note on the violin was; we still have those charts at home. It became an obsession with him. He used to play it on the trams, the old inter-urbans that ran between

Vancouver and New Westminster. He'd stand at the back, playing his violin on the way to work, just making use of his time." Gerussi laughs. "My brother and I would be going to work with him, and we'd sit way up front so nobody'd know we were connected with him.

"But later, when I was maybe fifteen or sixteen, I got really interested in what made him tick. He was a tremendously powerful man. In a rage he'd tear a door right off its hinges, but he never *never* laid a finger on Ma or any of the kids. He'd get terribly upset, and he'd go out and run as hard as he could for maybe two miles. I was doing track then, and I was pretty fast, but it was all I could do to keep up with him. I'd go and run with him, and then when he'd run it out we'd walk all the way back together and he'd tell me what was bothering him.

"But you see, there was no place in this dull, organized society for a man like him, and finally I guess he just packed it up. I remember going and seeing him in the hospital then—this fantastically powerful man—all the muscles in his face had fallen, his spirit just drooped. He jumped the fence that day and he walked all the way home—many miles—from the hospital to New Westminster, through the bush. He got home maybe 2.00 or 3.00 o'clock in the morning, had some food, and he just said, you know, that was *it*. I talked to him for hours and hours, said, Look, we'll get you out—

"Well, they came—the doctors and the police—and the next day he ran away again. It was months before we even found his body. But his bubble had burst, that's all. Too many pressures that he'd fought all his life, and he just wasn't going to have it his way. I *understand* that, there are lots of people broken by our society, by our system..."

What did that do to Bruno?

"I felt, and I still do, a deep resentment towards the authorities, the people in the hospital and the police—aw, Jesus—when it came to go looking for him there was just *no* help. The Mounties came round and said, 'Oh, he's probably in Nova Scotia.'

"That's what happens with institutions, you see? All humanity goes, and these people are just objects and numbers. Our society simply rejects the people we don't want. We put 'em in jail, put 'em in mental institutions, put'em in old folks' homes—get away—you don't belong to us any more. Well, that's *bullshit*: they *do* belong to us, they're our responsibility. I fight that dehumanizing process now, and I'll fight it till the day I die.''

Outside there's pelting rain and a gale of wind. As I drive away Bruno Gerussi waves, standing in his lighted doorway, a bright spot in the black night. Nice image, that. Maybe I can use it when I come to write about him.

(January, 1975)

An Elder
of the Tribe:

*This old cat I befriended
has somehow got it into her head
that I need looking after.*

"Well, I tell you," says Hubert Evans, leaning forward, a thin elbow on the arm of a cedar lawn chair, "I've taken to writing poetry. I never wrote poetry before in my life, but my friends think it's good. Of course that's no test."

*Even when I go to the bathroom
she tries to supervise.
Expelled, she mews:
"Are you all right in there?"*

A PORTRAIT OF

HUBERT
EVANS

"I got off on the wrong foot with poetry," Hubert explains. "Now my wife—all her life she memorized poetry—and at the end when she had a long and rather terrible illness, she could lie there awake by the hour saying it over, and she said, 'This is my library.'"

> *I know every nook and cranny*
> *of this old house—*
> *I should, I built it.*
> *But will she permit me to*
> *go from room to room*
> *unaccompanied? Not her!*
> *She makes my every move*
> *a personally conducted tour.*

"I'm ashamed to confess this," Hubert confesses, "but up till recently I'd never read any of Al Purdy. I think he's marvellous. Now that's the kind of writing I tend to, anyway, almost colloquial, but not quite. I'm writing as an old man, an old settler, about the things I remember."

> *Old cats are perceptive, granted.*
> *and maybe I do, at eighty-two*
> *"need help."*
> *But drat her! does she have to be*
> *so obvious about it?*

Hubert Evans is eighty-two, his eyesight is failing, and he sends atrociously cobbled-up letters to admirers like Margaret Laurence, explaining in a postscript that after over sixty years of hunt-and-peck typing he is teaching himself to touch-type. Hubert Evans doesn't want to sound like an old man, but he thinks I would quit smoking if I could really imagine what it was like last week, fighting to draw each breath in past the barriers of emphysema. His health doesn't permit him to go on the water much, but he loves to talk boats, having travelled the coast of British Columbia in cruisers and fishing boats he built with his own hands. He is eighty-two as the calendar flies, but not as the spirit meanders. The wattled skin hangs from his gaunt frame like wet sheets on a clothesline, and only one of his books is still in print.

He fought the 1935 troll strike with the other commercial fishermen of B.C., and he was one of the original organizers of the provincial CCF, and he wants to know about the Writers' Union of Canada.

"Now this is a great thing, this Union," he declares. "Back in 1927 someone told me I should join the Canadian Authors' Association, and I went along to a couple of their meetings. Well, I found these people just so *thrilled* that they'd had a poem published in *Chambers' Magazine*, or all so excited about getting something—I said Look, couldn't we hike the fee so that we'd get the *working* writers? But that went down like a lead balloon, I'll tell you. So I've never been active in it since. Now this Writers' Union is right along the lines of what I was suggesting thirty or forty years ago. What are your fees?"

"A hundred dollars a year."

"I can't afford it. No, I *can*, I can. I've got some money in the bank, I'm getting the old age pension; you put my name up for membership and I'll join." He laughs, a high, husky sound.

Really he should be an honorary member, for Hubert Evans was a professional writer when such elder statesmen as Ernest Buckler and Hugh MacLennan were in knee pants. In those days there was no Canada Council, there were no Governor-General's Awards, the universities had no writers-in-residence and the term "Canadian literature" smacked more of prophecy than description. That was before World War I, and Hubert Evans was a bright young reporter in Ontario.

He was born in Vankleek Hill, raised in Galt, and was always, he says, "an outdoor person. In my day, in the books, English boys ran away to sea. Well, it's a hell of a long run from Ontario to the ocean, you know? So I used to say I was going to run away up north and live with the Indians. And you know, as far as this French-English business is concerned, our *heroes* were the heroes of the Long Sault, the Jesuit fathers, Brébeuf and Lalemant, and a voyageur was to me what an air force pilot was to a kid in the first war years. *They* were the guys! I never had a bicycle, but by God I had a canoe as soon as I learned to swim. My father was a high school master in Galt, but he was a backwoods boy from Huron County, and his father was a famous broad-axe man, and– well–every year when school got out the whole family'd take off and go camping in the Muskoka country or the Sparrow Lakes or sometimes when times were tough maybe we'd just go in the back of some farmer's sugarbush. You know, all my life I can see a sort of essential philosophy emerging: travel light, have only the essential tools, but keep them sharp and know how to use them.''

He enrolled in forestry at the University of Toronto, but never attended; instead, he "just fell into newspaper work, the way most of us do." After a year on the Toronto *Mail and Empire*, he had a chance to edit a new morning paper in British Columbia, the New Westminster *News*. After a year on the coast, he went back to Toronto as city hall editor for the Toronto *World*. Then the war broke out. Evans enlisted, served in France, and was wounded at Ypres. He was eventually commissioned Lieutenant, and discharged back in Canada in 1919. His parents had moved to Vancouver; he had his job in Toronto, and a rail pass to visit them before he settled down.

"I looked at those old grey faces, the deskmen and editors at the *World*," he recalls, "and I thought Oh, no. No. All the way across the country I thought about it; it was March, you know, dirty snow, miserable. Well, on the train was Colonel F.H. Cunningham, who was Chief Inspector of Fisheries for the Pacific coast, and we had some drinks together–I thought I'd get a story out of him–you see? We got into Agassiz or Mission, I forget where, somewhere up the Fraser Valley, just after breakfast, and the old Colonel and I took a promenade on the platform, and in the station agent's little garden there was a plum tree in blossom, and there was a meadowlark on the fence post. Well, I took out the pass to Toronto, and I tore it up.

"We got back on the train and I said to the Colonel, What's the farthest north salmon hatchery you've got? I didn't know a thing about salmon hatcheries. 'Well,' he said, 'there's two, one in Babine and one in Lakelse, why?' I said, Because I want a job. 'What,' he said, 'at sixty dollars a month and your board? Good heavens, don't be crazy.'"

Cunningham was going to Europe for five years, trying to drum up markets for the cheaper grades of B.C. salmon, and he offered Evans a job as confidential secretary. But Evans was adamant. Ten days later he was on a train bound for Lakelse Lake, north of Terrace, a long way back in the bush.

"It was a wise move, though I've wondered sometimes since. They were going to build a new hatchery there, but it didn't get built, so the first winter I trapped in there with another wild man, and we had a very nice winter." He stayed there five years, and married a girl named Anna Winter. "The first requisite for a writer who's going to live the way we did is to marry the right woman, I'll tell you! My wife said she never wanted to marry a businessman: well, by God, she *didn't*. The first year I quit as a hatchery superintendent after six years in the bloody civil service – Elizabeth was only three, Joan was only a baby – I battered my brains out, and I made $96.00."

By then Evans had spent two years as superintendent of the hatchery at Cultus Lake, eighty miles from Vancouver, and he had built a house on a float – "a good float-house, it had a fireplace, a piano and everything" – and though $96.00 represented poverty even in 1927 the Evanses made out. "But you see," he declares, "within three years I was making the same amount of money as my father was making as a high school master in Vancouver. Until the Depression really hit home, it was *good*. The money was rolling in, and I was doing what I liked."

Between 1926 and 1930 Evans published six books, establishing himself as a writer for children as well as adults. Three of these books turn on the adventures of an Airedale named Derry; two are collections of that characteristically Canadian form, the animal story; one, *The New Front Line*, is, says its author, "a very naive novel." So it is, but that is only part of the truth. The novel tells the story of Hugh Henderson, returned soldier, and his distaste for the boosterism of the 1920's business life his parents wish for him. Instead Hugh visits a wartime buddy who runs a store and a little trucking business in the pioneering interior of B.C., and stays to homestead there himself.

Towards the end of the book, after Hugh has made his decision and married the local schoolteacher, the action becomes rather diffuse, as though Evans had lost his sense of direction. And admittedly the morality of the book is somewhat on the order of Boy Scouts and manly Christianity; its outlook is far from complex. And yet the book has a real charm; read in 1975, it also has some naive but powerful insights. Fresh from the trenches of France, Hugh finds modern life threatening.

"It should not be hard to sell people things they needed," Hugh thinks. "But instead there were people who wheedled or tried to bully the consumer by incessant suggestion into wearing or eating the particular article they had to sell, and behind these were unnecessary people of the second order. Their object seemed to be to complicate the growth, not simplify it. He remembered a statement in a full-page advertisement of a big American magazine: 'The luxuries of yesterday are the necessities of today.' True enough, but as you thought about it you asked yourself where it would lead. Was it tending toward some perfect existence or would it keep pyramiding until the whole structure of living became top-heavy and crashed?"

A good question in 1927. An excellent one today.

Hugh Henderson elects to stay close to real things, concrete things. So did Hubert Evans. He went on writing—"lived off *The American Boy* magazine for years, it was a sort of junior version of *The Saturday Evening Post*"—but he went on to build the house at Roberts Creek, where he still lives; he went logging (and wrote logging stories); he built his own boats and fished in the summers. "Two hundred dollars a month was my cash crop; but you could live like a *king* on $200 a month if you wanted to work with your hands, do some gardening, cut your own wood, build things. It was the life of Riley! And if you write something about me, this is the thing I'd most like to get across to young writers, that they *don't* have to make it big in New York. You can *still* have a wonderful life as a writer without a great deal of money. I tried it the other way for a year, once, living modern in the city, getting up in the morning and writing all day, with a little walk in the afternoon. What a hell of a life *that* was!"

When the Depression really struck, Evans went on writing, but he went fishing as well. "Do you know there was somewhere between 600 and 800 guys living out of rowboats in this gulf in the 'thirties, fishing salmon on handlines and living on the beaches? If a kid didn't catch a fish, he just bloody well didn't eat.

And the *camaraderie* between the hand trollers—it was all for one and one for all—it was really remarkable. These were guys from back east, from the Maritimes, rode the rods west, you know; one I remember was a judge's son. At the time R.B. Bennett was saying they were derelicts, but by golly, come the war they were being entrusted with Spitfires and Hurricanes.

"These were days when a guy in a rowboat would catch up to 140 salmon a day, on a handline! They'd live in shake shacks, or shanties made of driftwood along the beach. Some of them were the most improbable, most inept—I remember one guy, he'd been with the Mounties in the Arctic—a great big guy, a bull-headed, cranky fellow. He had one spinner—we used to make our own spinning lures, pound 'em out of brass, and his wouldn't fish worth a *damn*. He was going hungry, Jack Gavin was feeding him half the time—Jack was a Communist, by the way—and this guy held up his spinner and said, 'Those goddam fish will take that or nothing!' Well, they took *nothing*.

"Our whole family went. My wife taught our two girls and our son till they were twelve—she was about fifty years ahead of herself in education—and in three hours they got all the schooling they needed. When things were good we had a twenty-eight-foot cruiser with a little piano in it and slept aboard, this sort of thing; but when the magazines started folding, in the States particularly, you know, first the *Youth's Companion*, and then *The American Boy* and others, well then I went fishing in earnest. I started commercial fishing in '32, and kept at it about eight years."

By 1935, Evans was on the strike committee of the fishermen's union, when the Gulf of Georgia trollers went on strike. A hard-fought battle, it ended with the first signed agreement in the salmon fishery, a landmark achievement in B.C. labour history. The companies used every tactic to break it: racial divisions between the Japanese, the Indians and other fishermen, red-baiting, everything.

"I'm a queer mixture," Hubert says, "a Quaker but also a bit of an anarchist. Now come the revolution, where am I going to be? My good Communist friends have warned me, you know. Those were the fellows that took it on the chin in the '35 strike, the Communists. We were getting 5½¢ a pound for quality fish, you know, not netted but caught with a hook and line. Lasqueti Island is eight miles long, and along that shore there were eight scows and twenty-eight packers all competing for fish. When we went on strike there were kids hungry, and you'd get five or six fellows cutting up a fifteen-cent plug of tobacco, sharing it around. One time a packer came in and the skipper shouted, *Six girls aboard and free beer*! But nobody went near him. They sent up Navy patrol boats, and they went up and down offshore, offering 'protection' for any fisherman that wanted to go out and fish. Down in Vancouver the mayor, Telford, was on the radio saying the strike was only the work of a bunch of radical Communists, and he was a leader of the CCF himself!"

The CCF, of course, hated Communists. "Well, the Communists are serious and dedicated, and ruthless. No question they tried to break up the CCF clubs, but the only reason they came near to doing it was that the CCFers didn't come, you see? It's the same story in the unions: last summer there were 38,000 loggers on strike, but only 1,200 showed up to vote; the rest were all out fishing, or doing odd jobs or something. Well, it's easy for a determined group of people to take charge if most of the membership stays away, that's one of the hazards of the check-off. The price of liberty is eternal vigilance, always was.

"I was asked once or twice to join the Communist Party, but I said No, because I just don't believe that the end justifies the means. I went through a war to end wars, and look what the hell we've had since."

Evans was still writing, chiefly "serials," a now-vanished form somewhere between the magazine story and the full-length novel. How many of these he published is hard to say, but certainly a good number. The United Church *Observer* bought a 36,000-word story on the Depression, which none of the main magazines would touch; another church magazine, *The Canadian Girl*, published a series about the expulsion of the Japanese from the B.C. coast, one of the sorrier instances of Canadian wartime hysteria. "I've got an old feedbox out in the chicken coop that's *full* of published stories," Evans grins. He kept writing for children: in 1949 he published a fictional biography of the explorer David Thompson, *North to the Unknown*; in 1956 he published

Mountain Dog. But the work by which he is most likely to be remembered is his 1954 novel of the dilemma of northern B.C. Indians caught between two worlds, *Mist on the River.*

"When I was superintendent of the hatchery at Cultus Lake," he says, "there was a residential school for Indians six miles away, and my wife being the kind of person she was naturally got interested, and she went there and taught the day school for senior pupils. Well, I had a canoe and a skiff, and this float-house, so the older kids would come out on a Saturday and fool around, and I got to know them.

"During the war, one of our pupils—a fellow called Guy Williams, he's now a senator, a Kitimat Indian, shrewd as hell—he came to see us. I was in hospital. I'd put myself on the skids wrestling with a big log on the beach. I was a beachcomber at the time, recovering logs that had broken adrift from the booms. I was too old to go overseas, but I thought this was something I could do towards the war effort. 'Look, Mrs. Evans,' said Guy, 'the children of the children you taught haven't had a teacher for five years, up in Kitimat; they've forgotten how to speak English. Would you go up there?'

"I had seen Kitimat from the top of the mountains when I was hunting goats just after the first war, and I knew it was an old Indian village; this was long before Alcan and the smelter, of course. So we went up. Well, the whole village was out to meet us: what a reception! We went up there in December '44, and we were there two and a half years. By then our son John had to go to high school, so we went up into the Hazelton area, where there was a little one-room high school he could go to and be home week-ends. Oh, it was beautiful country, dry, back-east country, birch trees and all that sort of thing. We were there six years."

That country and that experience germinated Cy Pitt, the young hero of *Mist on the River.* Emerging into manhood, Cy is torn between the old ways and the old traditions of his tribe, represented by the memorable figure of the old canoe-maker Paul Leget, and the modern world of the English language, the cash economy, the business and technology into which Cy's sister June resolutely makes her way. In some ways the book is dated—nothing is so archaic as recently outmoded slang, for instance–but its images are powerful and moving, its language is supple and evocative. Indians come home to die of "the lung-sickness," vanish into alcoholism and prostitution, children die because the old medicine is not trusted and neither is the new. *Mist on the River* offers some remarkable love scenes: when Cy, a taciturn man, and his wife Miriam are fishing salmon in the stream, the event is suffused by sensuousness and fellowship. All the chief characters are Indian, and Evans is remarkably sensitive to their deep relationship to the land which has supported them for millennia, and to the dignity of their speech and thought. Indian society may be doomed, but white society comes across as shallowly opportunistic in comparison with the organic relationships among the Indians. Put the two together, Evans seems to say, give us the efficiency of white society and the humanity of the Indians, and you'd have a culture of real nobility. *Mist on the River* has its weaknesses, but at its core it is a thoughtful and deeply humane book.

"This was a labour of love," Hubert admits. "I was absolutely determined not to falsify anything for dramatic effect, not a damn thing, and I'm enough of a story-teller to know I *could* have. I sent it to two Toronto publishers, big ones, and they said, 'Good story, yes, but not of sufficient public interest.' Now this was twenty years ago–twenty-one years ago–and my wife said, 'The time is coming when that book will be recognized.'" It was published by Copp Clark, who were "looking for a bit of literary prestige," and it sold 3,000 copies at the time.

And now? At the Writers' Union meetings in Vancouver, Margaret Laurence leaned over to me and said, "A young friend of mine who's been spending some time with the Indians has shown me a damn good novel published years and years ago, it's called *Mist on the River*. Do you know it?" I told her I would be seeing Evans later that week. "Good heavens," she whispered, "I didn't think he could still be alive. Tell him how much I respect his book. He's really an elder of our tribe."

So I told him, and he laughed out loud, because Margaret Laurence is one of his favourite writers, and then he said the time had come for whites to keep out of Indian affairs and let them be worked out by the Indians themselves. "I would never," he said, "write another Indian book." Margaret Laurence wrote several books about Africa, I reminded him, but she would never write another, and for the same reason.

"Wonderful," said Hubert. He sank back in his chair and a shaft of sunlight burst through the clouds and into the kitchen of his daughter's home in West Vancouver, where he was recovering from his bout of emphysema, a frail figure in a white sweater, crowned with hair so white and buoyant it looks like spun glass. I thought about what I knew of his life, and it seemed to me it would not be so bad to be eighty-two if those years could be remembered as times of joy and gusto, of good work and good fellowship.

"I've never considered myself a great writer," said Hubert Evans. "But we're gettin' round to the Bible here, to the story of the talents. I have one bloody little small talent. And I thank the Lord that I have not wasted it."

When the ending overtakes me here
I will lie in this balsam-feathered bunk
draw the threadbare blanket over me,
and go, content.

(May, 1975)

Who's in Charge Here, Anyway?

This indolent lout Henry is snoozing in his chair before the TV, beer at hand, spatulate fingers splayed out across his vast, heaving belly. In the hallway, his rumpsprung wife is making a blasé remark about the new labour code to her obviously disgusted mother, and it's a funny enough cartoon.

But what brings the hoots and gales of laughter are the pictures on the wall. The one over Henry's head shows him asleep on an ottoman, cut off at the waist by the frame of the picture; the other picture, which peeps out from the wall of the foyer, shows the *other* half of him, his feet flopping over the *other* end of the ottoman. And just above his nose, hanging by a filament from a leaf of the potted plant, is a huge, hairy black spider.

A PORTRAIT OF

LEN NORRIS

"Well," grins Len Norris sheepishly, sipping a Bloody Mary, "if I've spent all bloody day on the thing, I'd like to hold the reader for longer than just a quick glance. So I put these little details in, just to hold him a bit. Give him something to look at."

Beer caps litter the floor. In the plant's pot, barely discernible, is an apple core. One of the mother-in-law's buttons is wildly at variance with the others. And her hat: her hat features a very scrawny, very angry, apparently quite *alive* bird.

"You try to make the details say something about the situation, too, as well as being funny in themselves," Norris muses, staring at the wreckage of his drink. "They don't make a very good Bloody Mary here, by the way."

That cartoon was published October 3, 1973. On November 6, the same characters cropped up in a similar cartoon, but seen from another angle. Two more pictures of Henry are visible, again with the head in one room and the feet in the other. A picture of his wife, however, has fallen from the wall and smashed on the floor. Everyone's clothes are the same, including the mother-in-law's animated hat. And the spider is *still* poised above Henry's nose.

"Something is always *going* to happen," Norris reflects. "You know, the picture is going to fall, the kid is going to saw off the table leg—a cartoon isn't restricted by things like the law of gravity, as a photograph is. So why not use that freedom?"

There's a curiously gentle ferocity in Norris' drawings, a feeling of improprieties bursting through polite conventions, a nice sense of the interminable battle against soot, falling pictures and general disarray. The tax collector arrives when you're in the shower. The goldfish glares back at you from his bowl. The cherubs which support your table lamp wear shocked expressions when you swear. A groovy, bearded psychiatrist visits a padded cell, in which you are locked in a straitjacket, and whispers, "Just between ourselves, your obsession that the rest of society is mad is probably true—but they are in charge."

Len Norris is conceivably the best-beloved institution in Vancouver, which is very odd, really; under the hilarious surface of his work lurks a distinctly mordant vision of life in Canada's Pacific wonderland. "He's a very gentle, thoughtful man, with a stiletto mind," opines Cliff MacKay, editorial page editor of the Vancouver *Sun* and thus the man to whom Norris reports. MacKay, who is about the size of a Centurion tank and who shakes your hand with a paw comparable to a very expensive roast, does not seem a particularly jolly or gentle soul. But he gets a funny little grin when he talks about Norris. "Len can skewer pomposity faster than anyone you ever saw. We think of him as our *only* resident genius."

Stephen Leacock once remarked that the news is only a rumour till you read it in your own hometown rag. Similarly, anyone who has spent years looking forward to Norris cartoons every evening will inevitably use them to measure all other cartoonists. It's a tough standard, and his colleagues know it. His office wall is festooned with appropriately inscribed originals from the Toronto *Star*'s Duncan Macpherson, from the scathing Montrealer Terry Mosher (Aislin), from other luminaries. The late Walt Kelly, creator of the immortal Pogo, called him "the greatest in the business."

"Rodney," says Norris through his chow mein, "Rodney's a fellow who gives me some concern, you know, that old British colonel type that crops up in a lot of my cartoons. I never look back at how I've done him before, and I think I probably do him very differently at different times." He does, in fact: Rodney's moustache is usually long, white and droopy, but at times it becomes bristly and even black; sometimes Rodney is very wealthy, at other times he seems a more or less standard English immigrant living on the daffy slopes of West Vancouver, where Norris himself lives, in fact.

Norris has a special knack for impaling the B.C. English, and over the years he has developed a whole mythological system about their habits and habitat. In West Vancouver, they while away their hours at the Amblesnide and Tiddlycove Cricket Club, fighting amalgamation with what one of them calls "the no-parking zone" across the First Narrows. They dominate Victoria, where they congregate in the Victoria Conservative Club and take tea at the Empress Hotel. Whereas Norris' Vancouver is a recognizable version of the city which lies outside his big office window in the Pacific Press Building, his Victoria is sheer fantasy, a squire's heaven, a tally-ho Disneyland where straight-backed women followed by packs of hounds ride blocky horses down the cobbled streets, where street signs point to "Crumpets" and to "Mid-Victoria."

Norris is himself English by birth, born in London in 1913. His style of cartooning, too, owes a good deal to such English cartoonists as Giles, Emwood and Trog; like them, he does not offer "editorial cartoons" in the traditional sense, caricatures of Uncle Sam and John Bull jousting over maiden Canada. He does not even offer identifiable politicians very often. Instead, he thinks of himself as a social commentator. "I get at the events from the viewpoint of the readers themselves," he says, "looking at how the news affects them."

He imagines, for instance, the kind of LIP grant which might be awarded in Rockbottom Creek, Norris' mythical backwater in the mountains of B.C. He samples economic programs from the viewpoint of the Akme Pewter Tuning Fork Company, watches Premier Barrett's ideas as they arrive in the body shops and fetid basement apartments of the working man, monitors the rulings of the CRTC from a prissy office-worker's living room. Over the years, Norris-watchers tune in and out of the continuing sagas of such figures as Rodney, Henry and a ferocious old virago in a long grey coat and an even longer black dress. She often plays bit parts, waiting in lineups and glaring down at her son-in-law from a picture frame on the wall, closing her eyes and twirling a knitting needle over her ballot.

"That old lady," muses Norris, setting down his coffee cup and lighting a cigarette, "just seems to turn up at all kinds of municipal events. I don't know why. She just seems to belong there."

What is it like to live in the path of an airport runway extension? It's like having blithe surveyors driving stakes through your living room floor. What do high interest rates mean? That counterfeiters find it more profitable to *lend* their produce than to pass it. How might a progressive mayor discourage private cars downtown? By hiring miniskirted girls to scatter tacks on the roads. What is the predictable result of tripling the family allowance? More kids, and kids are a plague already.

Norris' kids are a study in themselves. Squat, arrogant little brutes, at once sneaky and bold, they are diabolically shrewd. A predatory, pointed-toed moppet glowers up at her poker-playing father. "I don't care what they said at the Royal Commission on the Status of Women," he snaps, "Get back to bed!" An elaborately casual and sympathetic tad looks wide-eyed at his father, whose newspaper reports crises in housing, taxation, productivity: "Let's face it," he observes, "you've got a crummy report card." Kids lurk in the background of every other Norris cartoon, beating one another with logs of firewood, tickling the feet of sleeping soldiers, snitching apples, levering apart the house frame on which their parents are perched, pulling shrubs up by the roots, sinking their teeth gleefully into the spindly shanks of city policemen.

The first of Norris' horrible children was Filbert Phelps, the hideously imaginative son of a harried suburban matron and a sedentary taxpayer, and you can see him away back in 1951, in the first of Norris' twenty-three annual collections of cartoons. Filbert is the one who is setting the three sticks of dynamite under the desk, the one who rolled 237 cigarettes in his Grade 2 social studies class, the one who knows that his birthday dollar from Uncle Elmer in the States is worth only 99 and 31/32 cents. Filbert is the boy who *uses* the toilet in the Home Show, the boy whose good deed in Cubs is carrying a sandwich board which says VOTE FOR COCKTAIL BARS. That's Filbert running through the drapes with pinking shears, or pursuing his sister with an electric eggbeater.

"People always imagine my own children must have been just unbelievable little monsters," Norris chuckles. "But they weren't; they were just normal kids." The Norrises have two sons. One is an airline executive in Montreal–"the swinging bachelor of the family, who phones once a month and never writes"–and the other works for Crown Zellerbach in B.C. "They got into the usual pranks and scrapes that kids do," Norris admits, "but they were nothing like Filbert Phelps."

A prominent European psychiatrist named Freud once pointed out that humour allows one to say things which would normally be quite unacceptable. Norris' children are a perfect case in point.

98

Children are conventionally supposed to be innocent, charming, fragile and appealing, which indeed they are–sometimes. They are also boring, violent, cruel and cunning, just like real little people. You and I are not normally allowed to say so. But Norris does, every other day.

Freud also suggested that humour allows us to see the world freshly, without illusions, like a child. "We live in a society where policemen lift us from our cars to sniff our breath like some mediaeval winetasters," writes *Sun* columnist Allan Fotheringham, "where politicians soberly offer to bribe us with our own money, where we are bullied by clerks and civil servants and customs officers whose salaries we pay. We accept it and, by not complaining, perpetuate it. Len Norris, every day, points out how ludicrous we are and how ludicrous we look." Precisely: most often it is the reader who suffers under illusions, and Norris who sees things as they are.

"Vancouver," Norris marvels, "is great myth country. People here don't believe it gets cold, especially back in the 'fifties they didn't. It went down to *zero* the first winter I was here"–that's zero *Fahrenheit*: the year was 1950, when a miss was still better than a kilometer–"and we just about froze. Nobody had proper furnaces, they all had sawdust burners and no insulation. The *Sun* had found me an old place on West 14th, three storeys with a sawdust burner. The first week the bloody thing blew up, and I bought a house–*any* house!–just to get out of there."

Two years after Norris' arrival, British Columbia amazed itself and everyone else by electing a Social Credit government. For twenty years, provincial politics was a cartoonist's dream, and Norris created a mythical Social Crediter, an old-style carpetbagger with a wing collar, string tie, florid waistcoat and a towering, wide-brimmed hat.

"They were an incredible crew," Norris remembers, almost fondly. "Sanctimonious and corrupt." He shakes his head. Then he lights another cigarette and looks up. "Those high hats I always gave them were because they had to have room for the halos inside them. I don't know that anyone but me ever understood that was what they were for, but I kind of enjoyed it.

"But this bunch is just as mad. They're all mad, doesn't matter

99

which party you take. You get socialists tinkering with the economy, doing things for good reasons, and it so often turns out disastrously. Here in B.C. they froze all the easily-developed land, farm land, which was a good idea; but they didn't do anything to encourage development elsewhere. You see? From the best motives in the world the government has taken these ideas that look good on paper and *intensified* the housing problem."

Has he developed a New Democratic character to answer the old Socred carpetbagger?

"Sort of; he wears a paper cocked hat, you know, the old thing you used to make and wear sideways."

Leonard Matheson Norris came to Canada when he was thirteen; his father had a job in a pulp mill in Port Arthur. Then came the Depression, and the pulp mill closed down. The Norrises moved to Toronto, and Len weighed coal at the dockside for $12.50 a week. That led, curiously enough, to some commercial illustrations for the Elias Rogers Coal Company, and then, briefly to the Ontario College of Art, which left Norris massively unimpressed. Sardonic cartoons about abstract art and the pretensions of artists are a standard feature of his work. Ironically enough, however, he and Duncan Macpherson—whom Norris considers "just fantastic"—are the only two cartoonists in the Royal Canadian Academy of Arts, to which Norris was elected in 1974.

When the war came along, Lieutenant Norris of the Royal Canadian Electrical and Mechanical Engineers became editor of a service magazine called *Cam*, whose editorial policy, Norris recalls, was "preventive maintenance. They sent the damn thing to every unit that had any kind of equipment—motorcycles, jeeps, tanks—you name it. It was great fun, full of cartoons, comics and a sports-writing style." For his pleasures, the Army gave him an MBE, which he tries to conceal, claiming they were awarded more or less by the gross.

After the war, he took charge of artwork for such inspiring tentacles of the Maclean-Hunter octopus as *Bus and Truck Transport* and, later, *Canadian Homes and Gardens.* He was, he says, hopelessly caught up in the rat race, slogging away in the office all day and doing freelance work at night.

One of his chores about this time was illustrating the letters to the editor of *Maclean's,* of which the managing editor was then

Pierre Berton, lately arrived from the West Coast and, inevitably, the Vancouver *Sun.* As Berton tells it, *Sun* publisher Donald Cromie arrived in Berton's Toronto walk-up one day and asked where he might find a good cartoonist. A shrewd cookie even then, Berton extracted a bottle of rye and some baby clothes for his first child from Cromie in exchange for the name of Len Norris.

Well, um, said Norris. He thought it over for a year. Then the rat race finally became unbearable. "I wanted to play some golf and smell the flowers." When he reached Vancouver, however, Cromie was in the South Seas on a long vacation, and nobody knew anything about this retiring easterner who said he had a job on the paper. "Norris wanders around," says one observer, "behind this rummage sale moustache, and in a crowd of twenty people he'd finish twenty-first." He did some illustrations, started a comic strip for the *Sun* magazine (called "Filbert Phelps") and "drew maps for murder stories reading, 'X marks the spot where body was found.'" At the end of six months he was almost ready to go back to Toronto.

Eventually Cromie returned from the South Seas, or editor Hal Straight returned from Edmonton, or someone returned from somewhere and Norris finally got a crack at editorial cartooning. From there to here is a long straight record of growing fame, growing subtlety, and a string of awards. His annual volume is only distributed from Calgary west, but it sells out an edition of 27,000 copies. A year or two back he branched out to illustrate a children's book by *Sun* contributor Jack Richards, *Johann's Gift to Christmas.* Norris originals–which belong to Pacific Press, not to Norris–adorn Prince Philip's collection and the Vancouver Police Department mess. In 1973 he was awarded an honorary doctorate from the University of Windsor for reflecting, "with gentle humour, the hopes, the frustrations and the outlook of the average Canadian."

Not surprisingly, Norris remembers Donald Cromie with considerable affection. "He was an eccentric," he says, "but a wonderful guy to work for. You'd be sitting at your desk and a note would come from him. *I liked your work this month*, it would say, and clipped to it would be a cheque for maybe two hundred bucks. The Cromies bought a small weekly in Garden Grove,

California, and turned it into a daily. Gus Tierney was the managing editor, and Cromie said to me one day, 'Why don't you go down there this winter for six weeks? Change of pace, do you good.' So I went down, and Gus said, 'Where's your wife?' Well, I said, home, I guess.

"That's silly, said Gus, get her down here! So Marg came down on the next plane. Well, I showed Gus four or five roughs at the beginning of the week, and he said 'Great! I like 'em all!' So I finished them and spent the rest of the week playing golf. Things went on like that for the whole six weeks. It was quite a place, a bunch of little cottages on a ten-acre private estate, like living in a park. Well, I did this six-week stint in California every winter for a number of years. That was pretty nice."

Norris' day begins, he reports, with his "quiet hour," after he rises and brews a pot of tea at 7.15. He listens to the news, reads the morning *Province*, flips through magazines looking for ideas. He crosses to Vancouver after the worst of the rush hour, arriving at the office about 9.15. Aided by copious draughts of tea, he sketches and ponders until he has three or four roughs. At noon he takes them to Cliff MacKay's office, a few steps away.

"He presents you with some terrible dilemmas," MacKay grimaces. "He comes in here with three or four roughs and they're *all* brilliant, any newspaper in Canada would be delighted to publish any of them, and he makes you choose one and junk the others. No, he never fights for one over the others. In fact it's very difficult to get him to say which he likes. If you really press him, he'll maybe express a very mild preference for one or the other. He's a thoroughly responsible citizen."

I asked Norris whether he ever feels confined by having to submit his work to somebody else. No, he said, he and MacKay have worked together over twenty years, and they're good friends as well as colleagues. "I'm on page four, eh?" he explains. "And that's where the opinion of the paper is expressed. If I were on page six or seven I wouldn't want to show my cartoons to anyone; I'd feel quite free to express my own little personal prejudices—and we all have 'em—but page four is the opinion of the paper."

MacKay and Norris often lunch together, reviewing, says *Sun* publisher Stu Keate, "the week-end's golfing disasters." (Norris, according to Keate, "is a publisher's dream; a jewel. Conscientious. Unflappable. Loyal. A man of quiet dignity. A lousy putter.") After lunch, Norris goes back to work finishing the cartoon in all its uproarious detail. At 4.00 he drops the finished product off at the engravers, and goes home.

He smokes as though he were trying to alarm the fire chief and the cardiac specialists. He used to smoke three packs a day, often smoking three cigarettes at once when he was concentrating on his work. He apologizes for not offering a cigarette: "I'm just not accustomed to anyone else smoking. All my friends seem to have quit. I admire them very much." He doesn't think he could work without smoking, but after a heart attack a couple of years ago, he switched to a pipe.

"The pipe," he smiles, "is very economical, the doctor doesn't mind it, *and* it's a better smoke. I inhale cigarettes right down to my shoes. Now I smoke a package of pipe tobacco a day, though. I just happen to have cigarettes right now because I was up in the cafeteria this morning and I found I'd left my pipe down in my office. It was a perfect opportunity to go to the machine and buy cigarettes." He gives a despairing grin. "I couldn't *possibly* have waited till I got back to my office, which might have been all of ten minutes."

One of his more acerbic cartoons shows a sobbing widow talking to two mourners, in a living room full of consumer treasures: cabin cruiser, sports car, house trailer, surfboard, innumerable electric appliances, snowmobile, guitar, luggage. "I don't know what I'd do," she wails, "if he hadn't saved the cigarette coupons...rest his soul."

"My style has changed quite a bit over the years," Norris reflects. It has, too: the earlier Norris had a much less elaborate and oddly less realistic approach than he has since developed. And yes, he admits, beneath the celebrated gentleness, his work is often trenchant. "I'm a critic, I criticize everything. It's easy to do that, easy to be negative. Sometimes you wish you could go the other way; I make fun of the police, but when a policeman gets shot or something I'd like to do something sympathetic about it. But the medium doesn't seem to allow it."

How come he never runs out of ideas? Five days a week, fifty weeks a year, Len Norris finds something to be funny about. "I don't know," he says slowly. "I worry about that a little bit. But there always seems to be one more." Does he worry about repeating himself? "Yeah, I do. I probably *have* repeated myself, in the literally thousands of cartoons I've done over the years. I don't look back to see, though, and nobody has ever said anything to me about it."

As a matter of fact, in 1952 Norris did a cartoon of a man trying to beat the high cost of transportation by teaching his wife to ride a bike; twenty years later, he did an almost identical drawing on the same subject. the differences are instructive; the people look distinctly more like real people, the kids and dogs are even meaner, and Norris has become more adept at letting the reader know what he's talking about without resorting to a newspaper headline in the cartoon, or a News Item line at the top. And the feeling one often had in the early cartoons of the forest looming just at the edge of the city has almost vanished: instead of the woods, Norris' backgrounds now usually suggest skyscrapers. In that respect the change is in Vancouver as much as in Norris.

A great deal has been made of Norris' deceptive mildness; and it's true that he is profoundly a part of the society he mocks. Broadcaster Jack Webster calls him "a classic sheep in sheep's clothing." Listening to his soft speech, watching him shrug off praise, noting his self-effacing manner and realizing that he has not mentioned any of his honours, one is tempted to consider that true. But then you notice the eyes. They twinkle, it is true, and they reveal a genuinely friendly man. But they are as sharp, as penetrating and as observant as the lens of a camera, and they take note of things a camera never sees.

Consider the 1968 cartoon in which a sleek, portly executive of Akme TV Commercials Productions, Ltd., his desk littered with phones, confronts a bewildered, business-suited young black man who stands before him, hat in hand.

"Our policy here is not to use Negroes in our commercials," says the executive, "because we don't have a racial problem in Canada."

(April, 1975)

The Improbable Conscience of the CBC:

"Maryanne," said Keith Barry, program director of CBU, the CBC station in Vancouver, "you know what you're like? You're like Clare Boothe Luce trying to convert the Pope to Catholicism."

You may not know about Maryanne West, but Keith Barry certainly does. So do Laurent Picard, president of the CBC, and Pierre Juneau, chairman of the Canadian Radio-Television Commission. So does a good smattering of the CBC brass who inhabit the building on Toronto's Bay Street, the Kremlin, where the English network bosses hang out.

Maryanne West, you see, is a CBC listener.

Once upon a time she was a listener like thousands and thousands of others; a woman at home, raising a family in Gower

A PORTRAIT OF

MARYANNE WEST

105

Point, near Gibson's Landing, B.C., caring for an aged relative, listening with one ear to the Sony on the fridge while she fed the dog or washed the dishes. No more. Today she is the leading spokesman of a group called The Friends of the CBC; a director of the Canadian Broadcasting League; and an increasingly influential voice for a whole school of thought about the purpose and direction of the sprawling, infuriating and magnificent organization which annually spends several hundred million of your dollars and mine in broadcasting.

"Janey, get down!" says this increasingly influential voice. Janey is an elderly boxer dog much inclined to dispute the ownership of the comfortable chair in the fireside corner. She doesn't yield, so for the moment Maryanne shares the chair.

A comfortable old house, this, perched on the shoulder of a mountain, looking out to sea. Above it, enormous firs and maples sway, showering the sodden ground with the last vestiges of a black rainstorm. Inside, books from the Audubon Society lean against books by Gerald Durrell and other books on birds and nature. A cat, variously named "Tabitha" and "Dirty Old Man," wanders in, observes the dog with insouciance, and curls up before the fire.

"They get on very well," Maryanne explains. "We once had a raccoon named Tizzy, one of three babies some loggers found in a cut tree. We raised it for eight months, till it caught distemper and died. But the dog used to wash it, and it delighted in playing ambush games with the cat." She laughs. "I was going to write a book about it, but then I got entangled with this CBC radio business."

How did "this CBC radio business" begin?

"It began, I think, with the Radio One-Radio Two flap in 1971. The CBC planned to make the AM network a popular network–news, information, ads and what-not–and to put all the serious stuff over onto FM.

"Well, what hit us here, of course, was that My God, we're going to be discriminated against! We can't get FM! What also hit us was the reason they had been forced into doing something like this–the fact that they hadn't had the support that they should have had. We had taken the CBC for granted. In those days you could tune in to the CBC any time, and hear all these guys whistling in the dark, hoping that there was somebody out there listening to them. I don't think it *was* that nobody was listening to them, but nobody was *responding* to them, because up until then, well, my God, you don't write back to the radio, you know?

"So we knew it was partly our own fault. When you have a guilty conscience, that helps you to act. We understood what they were doing: they felt they had to rush out and try to make a popular radio that would compete in the marketplace."

Maryanne West had been in touch with Peter Gzowski, and on his last *Radio Free Friday* show he phoned her. "It was an emotional affair," she recalls, "because we were losing them, and we were losing so much at that time. For a whole week we'd been attending the burial of these various programs. Anyway, in that conversation it emerged that Warren Davis was going over to be the host of *Ideas*, which was on FM, and we wouldn't hear it.

"Well, that brought me a whole flood of phone calls the next day from people who'd heard the program, all wanting to know what we were going to do. So we decided to get together, and we wrote a brief. There were 200 names on that, all from this area, that we'd picked up in a week. I was just going to Toronto to welcome a new member of the family." The Wests have three daughters; one married in Toronto, one at Vancouver's Capilano College, and one doing archaeology in Afghanistan and elsewhere. "I took the brief with me, and spent some time with the network people there."

That pungent little brief pointed out that cultural facilities are plentiful in Vancouver but not so plentiful in the little communities of the Sechelt Peninsula, thirty or forty miles by highway and ferry from the city. Yet Vancouver gets FM, and the Sunshine Coast doesn't. The brief cited the 1968 Broadcasting Act, which calls on the CBC to be "a balanced service of information, enlightenment and entertainment for people of different ages, interests and tastes." It also cited the CBC's own brief to the Senate Mass Media Committee, in which then-President George Davidson said noble things about considering each part of the country "precious to the concept of Canada" and bringing each region "a lively appreciation of the distinctive contribution which it is capable of making; as well as an awareness of the richness that is added to its own life…by its close and intimate association with other regions."

Such fine words, Maryanne West declared to the denizens of the Kremlin, obviously buttered no parsnips. Her 200 listeners were losing half their drama as well as the news and reports from the BBC. Serious discussion and documentary programs were being shunted to FM and late-night AM. The country folks didn't feel all that precious. In fact, she said, we suspect you're looking for advertising and mass markets in the cities. That ain't what you're about. Get back to serving the people.

"They listened," Maryanne recalls, "but they were committed to the Radio One-Radio Two concept, and they had taken it to the Canadian Radio-Television Commission, who were about to hold hearings on the idea. So I came home, and we talked about it. We couldn't afford to send someone to Ottawa for the hearings, but we sent a brief–in fact we sent two–that first one and another we wrote especially for the hearing.

"Well, we were very heartened by the results, because most– no–I think *all* the points that we had made came back to us in the policy decision that the CRTC handed down. That's no particular credit to us, I don't think, because they were fairly obvious and they were said by people all across the country." The Radio One-Radio Two idea, said the CRTC, showed too much concern about ratings and not enough about "CBC radio's original function of reflecting to a national audience the total range of our living culture." The proposal catered unduly to the urban audience, and would tend to centralize program production. The CBC, said the Commission, *must* be distinct from private radio: "there is no need to spend public funds largely to duplicate what is already provided by commercial operations."

Victory!

"But one of the things we discovered at that time," Maryanne says, incredulously, "was that where *we* had started to holler because we couldn't get FM, *millions* of Canadians still don't get the full AM programming." Last September she made a swing through the Okanagan Valley, where CBC radio is only available through "affiliates," private stations which carry 15 per cent or

20 per cent of the CBC's AM programming. Today The Friends of the CBC have branches in Vernon, Summerland and Armstrong pressing for a proper CBC station in their own area.

A cheerful elf now assumes his place on the other side of the fireplace. He proves to be Frank West–Maryanne's husband–German by birth, British by anti-fascist principle, Canadian by eventual choice. He works as office manager at the Port Mellon pulp mill, serves on the local rural council, and scrutinizes the world through twinkling eyes almost hidden beneath enormous tufts of knotted eyebrows. "I see," he remarks, "that my wife has provided only one small ashtray. We have *two*." He peers at her. "In the matter of ashtrays, my dear, we can afford to be *lavish*."

The Friends of the CBC promote its programs by publishing a column of program notes in the weekly *Peninsula Times*. Realizing that the silence of listeners had helped cause the Radio One-Radio Two fiasco in the first place, the group makes a point of keeping in touch with the CBC production staff, letting them know what works and what doesn't, suggesting improvements, cheering them on.

That flexible, reciprocal relationship between the broadcaster and his audience accounts for Maryanne's deep admiration for what Peter Gzowski and his colleagues did in three years of *This Country In The Morning*. Conducting limerick contests, collecting recipes, phoning listeners who had written in, reading their letters on the air, *This Country* probably involved its listeners more deeply than any show in the history of Canadian radio.

"There's such a mischievous little boy in Peter," Maryanne observes. "There's nothing phoney about him, he's just himself, and a person like that comes across so well on radio. But Peter is the first to admit that what made *This Country In The Morning* was not so much Peter as the fact that everybody wrote back and that he *was* in contact with so many of us, that he knew who he was talking to. He wasn't just sitting in a little box in Toronto talking to himself, but he had this very close relationship with people all across the country."

The Friends of the CBC, in other words, did not dissolve once their initial crisis had passed. "It's a very loose organization,"

109

Maryanne explains, "because we don't want it to bog down in its own bureaucracy. We mostly operate by phone rather than holding meetings, and I've been the spokesman mainly because I've had the time. I've been involved before in publicity for the school board and this sort of thing, I can put together a brief, and so I've done the writing, to a great extent. But I do want it to be perfectly clear that there are a great many people working on this thing as well as me.

"And I really want to emphasize the CBC's need for support. You know, it's a national pastime to take swipes at the CBC, and God knows they have plenty of faults; but they'll only live up to their best selves when they know there are plenty of people around who realize their importance, who really support public broadcasting in this country and the men and women who spend their lives working for it. We really are *Friends* of the CBC."

The phone rings: it is for Frank, who plunges into a long conversation about a building permit. Hanging up, he reports that "that guy doesn't understand that he's got to get the building permit *before* he builds the house."

Despite the 1972 victory with the CRTC and the success of programs like *This Country*, the CBC still needs to be watched by its friends as closely as a mother watches a newly toilet-trained child.

"These guys are sincerely trying to cope in very difficult situations, I personally believe that," says Maryanne. "But you can't ever believe anything is dead unless you've personally buried it and are still standing on top, so you know nobody has exhumed the remains for re-incarnation. One of the Toronto brass, shattered by the fact that the CRTC threw out this new radio policy, was quoted in one of the Toronto papers as saying that he didn't care what the CRTC said, they were finally going to get this new policy pushed through. Certainly the philosophy that produced that proposal still permeates the CBC.

"You see, the CBC is trapped by this idiotic system, which isn't really public broadcasting. The CBC is sort of schizophrenic; they don't dare go right into public broadcasting, because they're afraid that then nobody will listen to them and their ratings will go down. And the government will say, 'Why the hell are we paying for this thing that nobody listens to?' And they'll be out. I

110

can very well understand their fears.

"But if the ship's going to sink—which is a real possibility, let's face it—I'd far rather it sank with all hands at their stations and standing for something, so that we know what we've lost, rather than see it sink because it can't compete in the marketplace and everybody says 'Aw, phooey, who listens to it anyway?'

"Another factor is that the guys who make these decisions live in the cities, most of them in Toronto, and if you're in Toronto, with twenty channels of television and God knows how much radio available to you, it's just beyond your capability to imagine what it's like when you *haven't* that range of choice. They won't get out into the countryside, either, though I've been trying to persuade them for three years. Do you know what one of them once said to me? *'What good would it do me to get out and meet all those people?'*"

Maryanne's country residence, in fact, lately made her a director of the Canadian Broadcasting League, a venerable grouping of supporters of public broadcasting. At a meeting in Vancouver, various people accused the CBC of being Eastern-oriented and ignoring the West. When they were done, Maryanne retorted that for country people Toronto is as relevant as Vancouver: both cities *equally* ignore you. The executive director of the League "was struck by the fact that here was someone from the bush, and perhaps they needed someone from the bush. And I notice with interest at directors' meetings that I do have a somewhat different attitude from everyone else, on almost every issue. They all live in metropolitan areas, you see?"

"It's like the ferry strike," Frank suggests. "Everyone is saying that if it happens it will cut off the Sechelt Peninsula. What nobody seems to grasp is that Vancouver itself will be cut off from what matters in the world, namely us. Do you have to go back there tonight? Ah!" He shakes his head. "You have my sympathy. You are going into exile."

Friends like Maryanne, people have remarked, are a thorny blessing to the CBC. But you have to understand her role. Though she has been a Canadian for years, she retains the remnants of an English accent; comfortably stationed in her fifties, her dark hair traced with grey, sporting a baggy polo shirt and blue jeans, she speaks with quiet humour, her ideas strung loosely along a thread of association. It takes a while to grasp that she is something like the CBC's house prophet, calling the faithless back to the ideals and principles which ostensibly provide the meaning of their lives, forecasting doom and destruction to the unrighteous.

She is certainly not much of a Friend to the moneychangers she presently decries in the temple. Seeking popularity by splitting CBC radio would debase the AM network, the one most Canadians can receive; reserving talks, documentaries, drama and satire, serious music and arts programming for FM means in practice denying them to most listeners. "The AM system is a mickeymouse network," Maryanne snaps, "but the FM 'network,' so-called, is even mickier-mouse, if that's a word. It doesn't *exist* outside the largest cities." As this is written, the CBC has not one English-language FM station operating east of Montreal.

"Would that be *mickier-mouse*, or *mickey-mousier*?" Frank inquires. "An interesting grammatical point."

"Either will do," Maryanne grins. "But look, the basic point is that the CBC can't survive *unless* it's public broadcasting. You can't be half-and-half, any more than you can be half-pregnant." She laughs, then turns the phrase further. "At the moment the CBC does behave as though it were running a trial pregnancy."

As a public service, the CBC provides important programming for a variety of minority audiences: farmers and fishermen, Indians, lovers of opera, gardeners and consumers, jazz freaks, stay-at-home playgoers and hockey fans. Nobody, perhaps, would savour everything the CBC may broadcast during a day; probably everybody can find one or two programs of compelling interest somewhere in the stew. For the CBC to be sucked into the ratings trap, Maryanne West argues, is to admit it's lost confidence in its own reason for existence. Playing someone else's game, it can only lose.

Does that really matter?

"Of course it does! *Of course it does!* The CBC is a vital part of the battle for our heads, on which the future of this country depends. People tend to think the CBC is secure behind the Broadcasting Act: that's totally naive. The Act could be changed by Parliament like *that!*" She snaps her fingers. "You see, the only

112

real security the CBC has is in the Canadian people, their belief in it, their insistence on having something that's distinctively Canadian. And that, I think, is something we need to think about. We don't always realize how important it is to cherish things, but it's been brought home to many of us in recent years. You know, that clean air and clean water we took for granted seems to have vanished overnight, that marsh we thought would always be there has been drained and a high-rise built; this country we have taken for granted may go the same way, and the CBC is part of that battle."

All right then, does *that* matter?

She looks at me, this improbable champion of a Canadian national broadcasting system, and in what was once an English accent she speaks very clearly and very forcefully.

"This Canadian mosaic," she says, "this Canadian experiment of all sorts of people from different backgrounds living together, is to a great extent unique in the world, certainly on the scale that we're doing it. And it's potentially of *immense* human significance, do you see? Because if we can do it, the rest of the world can do it too. We have to stay out of the melting pot, so that we can provide that example for all of humanity."

(December, 1974)

Dark Dreams on Main Street:

Nothing is as strange as ordinary life. The most unlikely people have the most surprising secrets. And history looks like a cigar box of papers.

Look at it: a Dutch cigar box full of scraps of paper. A sheaf of papers, each one numbered and bearing a different rubber stamp, each one about the size of a 35 mm. slide. Other documents on coarse, crummy paper, the kind you might find in wartime Europe, with official permission for this and that in languages I don't understand. Several mug-shots of one man, attached to several papers with different names. Coupons of some kind. An orange poster with heavy black printing on it.

The man's name is not Hendrik Dykstra. I will not tell you his

A PORTRAIT OF

HENDRIK DYKSTRA

114

real name. I found him on Main Street in a small town in British Columbia, in one of those offices in which men buy and sell automobiles, or land, or farm implements, or insurance, or television sets. Hendrik is industrious and thrifty; since he came to Canada in 1949, he has done well, as you can see when he takes you to his home, a roomy, carpeted split-level tucked among the trees on an ample lot. The fireplace is imposing. The fixtures in the bathroom are ornate. British Columbians generally are house-proud; the Dutch are good immigrants, and Hendrik tells you in a still-strong accent that he does not think of himself as Dutch.

He takes out his cigar box and tells you he does not want his name used because of the Werewolves.

Possibly no great war ever really ends. It is thirty years now since the last massive European nightmare officially ceased, but still the Israelis are hunting down the Eichmanns and Mengeles, and the survivors of the thousand-year-Reich are still hunting down the survivors of the various national undergrounds. With an appropriately Gothic flair, they call themselves the Were-wolves.

British Columbia is prosperous and curiously innocent. The subdivision is recently hewn from the forest; two cars stand in the driveway; no shadowy memories of history cast grim shapes into the future. *Je me souviens* is the motto of Quebec, *I remember*, but what Quebec remembers Main Street never knew—the rattle of gunfire on the farmsteads, conquest and subjugation. O happy province! Surely nobody here wakes up screaming in the night fleeing from lurid images of fire and slaughter, reliving the days crouched in hiding from the storm troopers who ripped apart the house?

This is March, 1975. Hendrik remembers March 3, 1945, and what he did on that sunny morning thirty years ago, in The Hague. He was holding a woman's hand.

"The bombs were still falling, and that wooman and her daughter were caught in between the debris—beams and iron and bricks. I could joost stick my hand through; I could see them, they were hiding away under a table which saved them, at that moment. They were completely encased in rubble and they couldn't get out. I didn't have the strength to do *anything*, I was

115

standing on a pile of stuff as high as this house. And I held her hand while they burned to death."

Hendrik's wife Elsa brings coffee-"or a beer? No?" Hendrik rummages in the cigar box. He has hardly spoken of these things for a quarter of a century: he has a new life, a new country, children who have grown up in the innocent forests and fields of British Columbia. And then, not long ago, they all watched a television documentary about the war and Hendrik had to tell them yes, it was as bad as that and worse. Yes, when he was their age, young, just into his manhood, he had been concerned not with cars and girls, but with Sten guns and survival. And yes, he had met Elsa through his work in the underground. Oh, he did have a few mementoes, an old cigar box....

"This," says Hendrik, holding up the sheaf of numbered rubber stamps, "is a catalogue. With correct papers, you could go anywhere, do anything, the Germans strangled themselves on their own papers. So! When we needed a paper, we contacted our documentation centre, chose what we needed from this catalogue here, ordered it and they made it up, so *good*, you couldn't tell it from the real thing. Say you had to smuggle an Allied airman out of the country: you had false papers made up for him, then you took him on the train to the border, and handed him over to the Belgian underground. And so eventually he would get out to Switzerland or Spain, and out to England. Some of them came through our hands two or three or even four times.

"We had three things to do, basically. First, we helped people get out of the country-you know-Jews, airmen, Allied agents and people like that. Second, we had to gather information about troop and vehicle movements, anything that might help the Allies know what were the Germans up to, and we sent that to London. Third, we had to help people endure as best they could, and to sabotage the German war effort wherever possible.

"We used to carry potatoes in our pockets, and when we got a chance, boom! we'd jam it up the exhaust of a German vehicle. They'd go a hundred yards, maybe, and then stop-an engine joost won't run without an exhaust-and the driver would jump out, put up the hood, look at the engine, scratching his head. Or we'd pour sugar in the gas tank; after that they'd have to overhaul the motor. Transport was very, very critical; if an army can't move it can't fight.

"Now these here, these are ration coupons. The Germans loved papers, okay, we reprinted them to death. All of these are forgeries, by the time we were done there were more ration books and coupons in Holland than people. These here are personal identifications, 'PB's,' we called them. I had three, all in different names, so I could immediately change from one face to the other. This one here is a guy that was dead; his death certificate was removed from the files, and my name and fingerprint put on the card, you see?

"We had agents everywhere, doing little things like that. We kept in touch by telephone; you had a list of numbers that you'd call, and when the call came in the operator knew what it was, and you'd be connected through a circuit the company didn't know about. Sometimes you'd have to call one number after another and another before you'd get through, because they had to change the numbers and circuits all the time."

Hendrik laughs. "You know, one time I remember we needed a small telephone exchange, and we didn't haf one, but the Gestapo did. So we watched the Gestapo headquarters for a few days, and we found they all went out for lunch; there was nobody in the office from 12.00 to 1.00. Well, my partner and I got all dressed up in Gestapo uniforms, and went in there at 12.05 one day, tore out the exchange, and got it out to the doorway. We had a truck supposedly coming at 12.15, and we were pooty nervous, I'll tell you, standing around in our Gestapo uniforms waiting for the truck, with our weapons in our pockets and our hands on the triggers. We waited, and waited, and the truck didn't come, we were pacing around and suddenly there was a BANG! and I looked over—my partner had squeezed his gun too tight—and shot himself in the foot! But still nobody came, and then at last came the truck, and the driver and I managed to muscle the exchange onto the truck." Then Hendrik helped his partner hobble to his bicycle, and they rode off to find a sympathetic doctor.

Hendrik's memories often combine comedy and horror. In those days, he says, he was in his early twenties, scared of nothing and looking for thrills; at times he sounds like a youthful prankster. He obviously boasted an icy nerve, perhaps because of that curious youthful illusion that nothing can *really* harm one. And yet unquestionably he saw many of his friends die, and was prepared to die himself.

"I remember one time my friend was in the documentation centre with another guy," he says, "and the Gestapo raided the house. Now we had our centre in a secret room off the basement, you see? It was concealed by a bookcase and things like that. They sat there for the whole day with their Sten guns and a box of dynamite, ready to blow up the whole house if they were found. The Gestapo tore the house apart looking for them, but somehow they missed our centre, and that evening they went away.

"So our guys were all right, but the documentation centre had to be changed if they knew where it was. Now this thing there"– he reaches into the cigar box and pulls out an armband, validated with a rubber stamp–"is an armband that permits you to be on the street after the curfew. So that night we went back, got into the house through a back window, took the stuff that was essential and destroyed everything else. We got everything loaded in our cart and started out down the street in our Gestapo uniforms and then we found coming down the street was the Landguard, these were Dutch people who worked with the Nazis as street patrolmen and things like that.

"Well, I thought, *This is it*, you see? Here we were with this whole handcart full of stuff from the documentation centre, and I thought we'd had it. But Jan whispered to me, *Leave this to me*, and he marched straight over to the Landguard and demanded to see *their* papers! He questioned them very severely: were they who they said they were, what were they doing here, were they supposed to be in this part of town, you know, that kind of stuff. They were pretty stupid anyway as a general rule, the Landguard, and he had them shaking in their boots. After a while he let them go, and we went on our way with all the rubber stamps and documents and stuff."

I believe it was Mao Tse-tung who said that the guerilla moves among the people as a fish moves within the water. Throughout Holland the underground had its contacts, people who would falsify a document, repair a radio transmitter, shelter a fugitive. An airman would be shot down and taken in by a farmer, who would mention it to someone he knew was in touch with the underground. The word would pass along until one day the airman would be taken in tow and whisked off to the border. What about the fact that they didn't speak Dutch? "Get 'em in the toilet when their papers are checked," grins Hendrik. "Or have 'em pretend they're asleep." One day a woman and her daughter showed up at Hendrik's father's office, where Hendrick was ostensibly employed, to let it be known that they were sheltering a draft-dodger, and needed extra food.

"I didn't admit I knew anything about the underground," says Hendrik, "but we checked out the whole thing, that it was true, and then we started taking bits of food to them when we had it to distribute." To this day, the daughter remembers the unnerving way Hendrik would suddenly appear: "We left the little grille open in the door," she explains, "so that he could reach in to the latch. But he came in so *silent*! We would be sitting there in the dark in the living room, during the blackout, and suddenly Hendrik was just *there*, maybe with a bag of beans for Pieter. Nobody heard him come, nobody heard him go, he was like a ghost." The daughter's name was Elsa, and for thirty years she has been his wife.

"It's not so bad now," she says, "but when we were first married, Hendrik would have these terrible nightmares, shouting in German and fighting with the Gestapo in his sleep, and I had to move the beds apart, you know? I was afraid he would *kill* me in his sleep."

"I don't dream about it much now," smiles Hendrik, his blue eyes crinkling. He is balding, fifty-fiveish, angular and bony despite the svelte lines of an expensive blue tee-shirt and a pair of check slacks. A man from Main Street.

"Tonight," says Elsa, "tonight I move the beds apart. After all this talk about the war?" She casts her eyes to heaven.

Cheek by jowl with the Nazis in a crowded European city. Striking your small blows where you could. Cranking the pedals of a bicycle upended on the living room floor, so that its disconnected generator could be used to power an illicit radio. Lying on a mattress in an attic, three of you with your Sten guns, while the Gestapo prowled the house below. Watching and being watched.

"Next door to us," Elsa says, "for *three years* there was a Jew hidden, a young man, and he never left that room. He even went to the bathroom on a piece of paper so nobody would hear the plumbing running and be suspicious. After the war was over he came to me and said, For three years the only joy I had was watching you and your little brother playing outside in the garden, thank you so much. He used to stand back from the window where nobody could see in, but he could see out."

The row house next to Hendrik's parents was taken over by the Gestapo. Hendrik and his partners went out to the country one night for a weapons drop. Down came the British plane over the farmer's field, and flashed its lights; the ground party put on its answering lights, and the parachutes of weapons floated to the ground, to be collected quickly and taken into town.

"They were in big metal containers," Hendrik remembers, "all packed in grease, so if they landed in water they wouldn't be damaged. They were all in parts, so we took them to my father's basement and wiped the grease off them, but we had never seen any guns like them before. They were the first Sten guns we got, and we didn't know how they worked. We tried to put them together, which piece fitted where, and how to load them and all of a sudden *bu-bup*! like that—one had gone off—and shot my friend in the boot, you see? with the Gestapo in the next house, on the other side of the wall! But they didn't hear it."

I get the impression the Dutch underground spent a lot of time shooting itself in the feet. Hendrik grins.

"Yeah, twice anyway. But a different man's feet."

Papers: in the early part of the war, so much of Hendrik's war was a battle of papers. "A PB identification for a Jew," he explains, "had a big J printed right into the paper of the card. And you know we had people so skilled they could cut that J right out, just the thin top layer of card, and replace it with the same kind of special paper so accurately you wouldn't know the J was ever there?" The document people one day gave Hendrik a splashy identification paper with a big red seal on it. "We don't know what this is," they said, "We only saw the first one like this the other day. But take it, it might come in useful." Hendrik had it when he was hauled off a train one night, returning from the border with his pockets full of forged food coupons, foreign money and forged papers.

"The Gestapo did not trust my identification," he says, "and they took me off the train and took me to see the two top Gestapo officers in Holland–two men we were very scared for–I knew them very well by name. They looked at my papers, and then Muller looked at this other identification, and asked what was it? I said I didn't know; that it had been given to me by my superiors for whom I was working as an administrator, to be used in time of emergency. I was anxious to get out of there, but instead I was put in a van with some other prisoners and driven to the Orange Hotel; that's the name given by the underground to the largest penitentiary in the old country.

"Well, then I was searched, and eventually they found the envelope full of papers, which I had slipped into the lining of my coat while I was waiting. But I made a remark that the pocket of the coat was kaput, and they really didn't look very hard. Oh, food coupons! Yeah, I said, food coupons. Anyone who knew anything about food coupons would know I had far too many for one single person to be carrying, but this particular searcher wasn't too smart."

Hendrik spent the night in a cell–in new pajamas, he recalls, which impressed the guards; he had intended visiting a girl friend that night–and in the morning he was released. As he walked out of the high-security zone, he kept waiting for the shot in the back which would make him "killed while attempting to escape." It never came. He had orders to report to Gestapo headquarters, and after conferring with his father, he did.

"Two fellows tried to interrogate me again, and eventually they brought up this particular identification paper again, and asked me again what it was. I told them I didn't know, and I could see it in their faces that they didn't know either. Later on I decided that they thought it was from another secret office about which they had no knowledge, and rather than take a chance on interfering with something that might get them in trouble, they let me go. They said, 'But you don't need this,' and before my eyes they tore up that paper. I still don't know what it was, but I'm sure it saved my life. I was the last member of the underground to come out of the Orange Hotel alive."

After that the underground was suspicious of Hendrik himself—as he says, "to come out of the Orange Hotel, that was joost something that doesn't happen"—and he had to be kept out of sensitive positions. He was reassigned to the military wing of the movement, hijacking food, sabotaging German facilities, disciplining black marketeers.

"This orange poster here," he says, pulling it out of the cigar box, "this is what we used with black marketeers. By this time in the war things were getting very bad. The last week of the war, I remember, our rations were, for every citizen, one half-loaf of dirty, stinking bread, and one box of matches."

"I remember once," Elsa grimaces, "coming home and finding my mother frying beets in some kind of motor oil."

"You see what kind of a position this gave to a farmer?" Hendrik demands. "A farmer had *food*—and some of them took advantage of it. I remember our little group one time raided a farmer that we heard was selling on the black market—he could get anything from the people, Persian rugs and silver and jewellery, for just a few eggs or a bit of milk, and he did. So we raided him one night. He was brave, and he was strong, I'll say that, it took eight of us to bring him under control. Then when we had got the stuff we took it and distributed it to people that were hungry, and on our way out we put these posters on his fence, to say he had been disciplined by the underground for black marketeering. He took them off, but people saw them before he got them down, and everyone knew what had happened."

Another raid on a barge full of potatoes was less successful; some of the raiders were nervous and started shooting when the guard approached. Two of Hendrik's closest friends were killed. "In the last two years of the war we lost an awful lot of men," Hendrik says sadly. "The Germans were desperate, and they were getting on to us. They'd find a young girl that we were using as a courier, and they'd follow her for a week, and then they'd make a sweep. When the war ended the local Gestapo had a list with forty-two men on it, names and addresses, different hiding places. They were going to raid us the next week. My name was on that list."

Probably the most horrible of his memories is The Hague bombing in March, 1945, the day he held a woman's hand while she burned to death.

"You have a famous park in The Hague, and we got knowledge that the Germans were preparing that particular park for a V2 rocket installation. We relayed the information to England, and they came back and asked us for markings, orientation points, as to where this park was. They could have gotten lots of information in England, mind you, because there were lots of people there from The Hague. But we told them there were two churches with towers, and that they should locate on one church, and we mentioned the name of the church, so that they could check on it.

"Of course the Americans and the British couldn't afford to let this V2 station stand – it was in use – the rockets went up regularly." He chuckles. "Came down, too, sometimes nearby. So one night we got word: it's going to be tomorrow. And in the morning in come the Americans with all those Flying Fortresses; *and they take the wrong tower.* They bombard one of the most populated sections of The Hague. And I tell you, they *bombed* it. Then the Spitfires came in.

"In the meantime the fire trucks came out – but they didn't have any gasoline – so they were horse-drawn, and the Spitfires swooping in and shooting up the horses. Then they put that jelly on, the stuff that burns. You have never seen it, street after street – I have actually seen it – that this side of the street is on fire, and you have a howling wind, and then suddenly the whole wall of flame arches over and the other side is on fire, and people running in between. I have seen when those horses got shot people slashing them apart with their knives to get meat, while in the meantime the Spitfires were just strafing the streets."

He is a long way away now, in another life. His accent is more pronounced. He falls silent, and Elsa talks about her own experiences that ghastly day, the Spitfires and the flying glass, the woman gurgling to her death with a slashed throat, the back of

Elsa's knapsack bursting into flames.

"Do you know what happens to body," Hendrik demands, "when you're close to bomb explosion? You won't believe it. A body, a complete natural body, is reduced to a pile of mud that high." He holds his hand perhaps ten inches from the floor. "I stepped on them. I've seen women–I knew they were women because of their dresses–in a bubble that size. And I stepped in them, not knowing what it was. It's the concussion that does that. I don't like to talk about it.

"And the irony was, within the hour another V2 went up."

Nothing is as strange as the quiet life of Main Street. The most unlikely people have the most surprising secrets. And history looks like a cigar box full of papers.

(May, 1975)

Pacific Anarchist:

The anarchist crouches in alleyways, with his red-rimmed eyes flicking this way and that, clutching his bomb. The anarchist is violent and fanatic, the slave of an obscure ideology spawned in the black backwaters of European history. The anarchist stands for a return to the jungle, for a complete breakdown of civil order. The anarchist is a savage. He eats babies. Right?

Wrong. One of the most prominent anarchists in the world is a pacific sixty-three-year-old man of letters who lives quietly in the Kerrisdale district of Vancouver. Every year he pours out a torrent of books, articles, plays and poems. He is addicted to travel, and periodically vanishes on six-month visits to India, to Europe, to the South Seas. He receives a modest stipend from the Univer-

A PORTRAIT OF

GEORGE WOODCOCK

sity of British Columbia and edits the quarterly journal *Canadian Literature*. He writes documentaries and talks for CBC radio and television; and if you have gone a year without seeing or reading his work, you are a sleep-walker. His name is George Woodcock, and he is quite possibly the most civilized man in Canada. He has never eaten a single baby.

"Anarchism," smiles George Woodcock, "is a doctrine which recognizes that man is not good by nature, but *social* by nature, and that the basic social forms arise naturally out of human intercourse; and that the more we try to regulate them, the more we try to govern them, the more we pervert them. A certain amount of violence is inevitable in human life, but it is *increased* by the inhibitions of government. If you have freedom, you're much more likely to have peace among people, you're much more likely to have natural forms of social organization."

If we want to know more—and I think we do—we might look at Woodcock's *Anarchism*, the standard book on the subject, available in paperback. If we want to know about anarchist tactics, we might pick up the collection of his radio talks, *Civil Disobedience*. Or we might consult biographies of the anarchist activists, theorists, and sympathetic men of letters—William Godwin, Mohandas Gandhi, Pierre-Joseph Proudhon, Prince Peter Kropotkin, Oscar Wilde, George Orwell, Herbert Read. We might look into such related enterprises as the Doukhobor ideal of a simple communal life in harmony with God and nature. Woodcock has written books about all of them.

Woodcock has written, he admits, "forty-odd books"; there is even a book about Woodcock, by Peter Hughes, who points out that Woodcock "has written more than many literate people have read. In a recent twelve-month period, for example, he published four books and thirty-three articles and reviews. His subjects range from Persian history, poetry and fiction, Canadiana, political theory, education, and Mao Tse-tung." Perhaps even more astonishing is the fact that all his work is at least competent, and large stretches of it are brilliant.

"Well, it's a matter really of just keeping one's hand in," Woodcock explains rather diffidently. He sits in a cubicle of an office in the UBC auditorium, perched somewhat uneasily in his chair. Polite, quietly well-groomed in his fresh striped shirt and sports jacket, his white hair and pink complexion giving him something of the air of a mature cherub, he speaks easily; he doesn't tell me he's uncomfortable. Instead he writes it, in a diary excerpt published in *Northern Journey.*

> Fetherling, writing in *The Globe and Mail*, remarks that I was hesitant and reticent when he tried to get information out of me. In fact I was downright evasive, as I always am on such occasions. Why? Once I was childishly open with my feelings and found that hearts on sleeves invited knives, and became taciturn about revealing anything inward...except indirectly, in poems, in plays, in biographies where I can march my boundaries with the subject.

He says nothing of this: I have to find the piece and read it. "I never like to talk much about my books after publication," he writes, "and always evade interviews, because *it is all there for those who can read.*"

So we meet at the office, not at home, and though Woodcock is as courteous and cordial as one could wish, I come away feeling that I knew him pretty well before we met, and my opinions have changed very little. In 1964, Woodcock accepted the first essay I ever published, and chose to reprint it in one of his 1975 books; later, when I was an editor, I published a pair of splendid essays by him. We have been in touch many times in the past ten years, by mail or by phone, and we regularly read one another's work. At last we meet, and that is a curiously unimportant pleasure. *It is all there for those who can read*: Woodcock gives one plenty of reading.

"I probably don't do more than three or three and a half hours' real writing a day; much else goes in reading, letters, going off for a walk, doing all the other odd things I have to do. But if you keep on doing three or three and a half hours a day over a year, you produce a lot in the end. And I'm fortunate in that I don't have to revise very much; I do one draft, revise on the draft, re-type it and that's it; I don't have to work things over time and again. It's just a natural sort of facility, I guess.

"I enjoy it, I'm sort of fanatical about writing. I started as a poet, actually, and recently I've gone back to that, I'm hoping to get a few things together into a book. But I have—I suppose I have—an extraordinary curiosity; I can't keep from learning about things, and once I've learnt about them I want to write about them. Mind you, the topics do interconnect. An interest in literature and an interest in radical politics come together and produce an interest in radical literature, more than other literature. And from that, things do spark off. I go to India because I'm interested in Gandhi, but then I get there and I find that all the little details of Indian life interest me vastly, so then I really write a book which is more about village life and town life as you see it from day to day than about Gandhi. Later on I do write a book about Gandhi, of course, which is also part of the sequence.

"But then when I'm there I get interested in the evidences of the Greek invasion of the Punjab in the centuries after Alexander, and I write a book called *The Greeks in India*, which was the first of its kind. And so things sort of go from one to the other, but there's usually a connecting link, a thin line that connects all the interests."

But these are curious interests in a life which began in the raw boom town of Winnipeg in 1912. Woodcock's father came to Canada from his native Shropshire in 1907, a servant's son seeking his fortune in the empire of the West. He worked as a hired hand, lost his health, and returned to England a few months after Woodcock's birth. But in the twelve remaining years of his life, he talked endlessly of the life and vigour of the Canadian frontier—its climate—at once demanding and beautiful; its people, polyglot and vital; shootouts on the streetcars and Charlie Chaplin on tour; Blackfoot and Cree, Chinese and Doukhobors. "Always, like a mirage above the Shropshire and Chiltern landscapes in which my childhood passed," writes Woodcock, "there floated this memory country which my parents' talk constructed, until the land I had left when I was less than a year old seemed to have become a part of my own memory, its scenes imagined vividly and imprinted on my mind with an accuracy which I found astonishing when I later travelled over the actual soil of the Canadian Prairies."

Woodcock's accent is still distinctly English, despite his years in Canada. "My first job," he remembers, "was as a clerk on the Great Western Railway." He pronounces it "clark."

"My grandfather, who was a fairly well-to-do coal merchant in Shropshire, offered to send me to university if I would become a clergyman, an Anglican clergyman. That was my first act of rebellion, was to say No. That was why I never went to university, because in England in those days, unless you got one of the very rare scholarships, you couldn't; even with a scholarship it was hard to afford it unless you had some form of private means. So I had no university education—I'm not sorry, really, in a way—and I picked up other things in different ways."

That's right: George Woodcock, one of our most learned men, sometime professor of English, world authority on a number of scholarly topics, historian, critic, poet and philosopher, George Woodcock has no university degrees at all, aside from honorary ones.

Instead he had a decade which he remembers as "the uncertain years which are dimmest in my memory, far dimmer than childhood, the nine-to-five years, a decade of sub-bureaucratic drudgery, lit by black fires and frustration in whose anti-glare I clung to the crumbling ledge of 30 shillings a week, as one did in the 'thirties if one's fingers held. Depression Years personally as well as collectively." He had thought of becoming a naturalist like Henry Walter Bates, whom he read in his teens and upon whom (naturally) he has since written a book. But science had passed beyond the point where it easily merged with literature, and for a dozen years Woodcock laboured in a variety of jobs, saving money, hoping to be free by the age of forty to live frugally in the country and to write.

Meanwhile he was already writing constantly: diaries in which he recorded not only what he saw, thought and felt, but also details of the reading which constituted his home-made education; poems; and three novels. He burned them all. By then, he says, "I knew everything about how a novel should not be written, and found I had no desire to continue. Yet in the process I had acquired the primary equipment of a critic: to know the pains of creation, the reasons for failure."

A combination of good luck and good management liberated

him for full-time writing at twenty-eight, a dozen years ahead of schedule. At nineteen, he had become an anarchist: "in an otherwise empty railway compartment near Oxford a page of Kropotkin changed the direction of my life." In his late twenties, he moved into the complex web of little magazines and personal friendships which characterizes literary London; he became friends with poets such as Julian Symons, Roy Fuller and Kathleen Raine, with libertarian writers and thinkers like Herbert Read and George Orwell. He edited a literary magazine, *Now*, and had a hand in the anarchist publication *Freedom*. He published some books of poetry and, in 1944, his first prose work, *Anarchy or Chaos*, a work which now seems to him "embarrassingly doctrinaire."

In the meantime, of course, there was a war going on. To a socialist, wars between capitalist governments are not the stuff of which crusades are made; to a libertarian, conscription is particularly revolting. Woodcock, who often describes anarchism as "libertarian socialism," spent three years dodging the draft. As England emerged from the rubble into the gloomy austerity of Cripps and Attlee, Woodcock grew more depressed. In 1949 he married, and came with his wife to the country in which he was born, the country of his father's compelling memories.

Imbedded in the anarchist tradition is a dream of living by a combination of manual and mental work, in a harmony which recognizes both sides of human nature. The Woodcocks tried it. "We took a piece of land on Vancouver Island and built a house ourselves, with our own hands, never having done anything of that kind before. Then I went away for a year and came back, and we built another house." They kept a few animals, planted crops, tried to create a subsistence farm. "It was a very interesting experience: one learnt a great deal. One learned that it was possible to acquire all sorts of manual skills, with a little intelligence and a little application, and that was very gratifying. But it also taught me that although the anarchists have always held that to be the ideal, balancing intellectual life and manual work, it's a matter of temperament essentially, and that I didn't have the temperament for it. Oh, I still like even now to do a little gardening, a little carpentry—for a variation—to use my hands now and again. But the idea of trying to marry the two on a more or less equal basis is for me hopeless."

Coming to Canada seems to have rekindled Woodcock's long desire to travel: in 1952 he published *Ravens and Prophets*, a book of travels in Western Canada, the first of many travel books. At about the same time the Woodcocks moved to Vancouver, living at one time in a cabin on Capitol Hill. "At that time it was almost the only house on Capitol Hill; it's now, of course, all suburban villas and this kind of thing, but then it was quite pleasant, pheasants outside the door and a fine view looking down on Vancouver." At the time Woodcock was living entirely as a writer, doing CBC talks, articles and reviews for a variety of publications in Canada and elsewhere; it was a slender time.

In 1954, Woodcock went to Seattle, where he taught for a year at the University of Washington; the University of British Columbia, which had been hesitant about hiring a man with no degrees, took heart and employed him as an associate professor from 1956 to 1963. He taught European literature in translation: Tolstoy, Turgenev, Stendhal, Flaubert, Proust, the great names of the European nineteenth century. I was an undergraduate at the time, and I remember that the course didn't count towards a major in English. Never mind, another professor told me, "one reads those books anyway; one doesn't need a course in them." I allowed myself to be persuaded. Twenty years later I still regret it, and I still haven't read a good many of the books Woodcock discussed.

In 1959 Woodcock became the founding editor of *Canadian Literature*, which has now published sixty-odd fat issues and long ago established itself as the main outlet in which Canadian critics could discuss our developing literature. Elegantly designed and printed, *Canadian Literature* is one of the few academic quarterlies you can actually read without inducing headaches and stomach trouble. For that readability, Woodcock's taste as an editor is largely responsible, and the magazine has both fed upon and encouraged the remarkable growth of Canadian criticism in the last fifteen years.

In 1963 Woodcock wanted to go travelling again, and the university refused to give him a year's unpaid leave. "They were very strict on leave at that time, for some odd reason," he smiles, "so I resigned. Roy Daniells, who was head of the English department, was very perturbed about it, and said, 'Well, isn't there some way to arrange it so you can carry on the magazine?' In the end I was re-appointed as a part-time lecturer, just to give me some kind of title, to edit *Canadian Literature.* That suited me very well, actually; I'm here on a part-time salary, and I have plenty of time to write and travel."

He taught again in 1966-67, but a heart attack mid-way through the year forced him to give it up. He had agreed to teach a course on Indian literature in translation, but hadn't counted on the amount of reading it would require, and he found himself overworked. But the more important problem, he believes, was that "though I enjoyed teaching, basically I resented it, because I found that when I was teaching I was really letting off into the air all the kinds of things I should be writing. I'd be up there on the podium and I'd deliver a lecture in which I'd say about fifty different interesting things about Gide, which I should have been putting into an essay. But when I'd said them I had no real incentive to write them down. So really good ideas were being lost in the air all the time, and I think that's possibly part of the cause of my illness."

All the while Woodcock continued his travels–to Mexico and Peru, to India and Polynesia. The books poured forth: *To the City of the Dead; Incas and Other Men; Kerala, a Portrait of the Malabar Coast; Asia, Gods and Cities; Faces of India; The British in the Far East.* Literature was not forgotten: in 1966 Woodcock received the Governor-General's Award for his biography of George Orwell, *The Crystal Spirit.* Canada was not forgotten: in 1968, with Ivan Avakumovic, he published *The Doukhobors,* easily the best book on that troubled and inspiring people, and two years later published *Canada and the Canadians,* suitably dedicated "to the memory of my father, who never came back." Two years later again he published *The Rejection of Politics,* a collection of essays on "Canada, Canadians, anarchism and the world." Yes, Herman, there *is* a touch of wry egotism about that. In 1973 he won the Molson Prize of the Canada Council, which recognized not just one book, but a lifetime of distinguished work in the arts.

132

Woodcock has a couple of considerable advantages, notably his wife. Inge Woodcock, says her husband, is a voracious reader, a potter, and "a very good linguist. German is her native language, and she speaks Spanish, Italian–she's very good at picking up enough to get along with, too. She's one of these people who can go into a country and in a month get a fair smattering of the language. She's particularly interested in Tibetan language and literature." The Woodcocks, in fact, were for many years among the pillars of the Tibetan Refugee Aid Society, set up to assist the Tibetans who fled their country when the Chinese invaded it.

Woodcock also has at his disposal an eminently readable style which moves with equal ease among the abstractions of political theory and the concrete details of people and places. "The Depression," he writes, "closed down over my youth." Yes, exactly. "The burning leaves of the vine maple are beginning to fall and the geese are crying southward over the mountains sugared with first snow." Often his crisp precision rises to a kind of elegant wit. "Canada's Senate is probably as hospitable a stable for dinosaurs as America's, but our dinosaurs are safely fossilized, whereas in Washington Tyrannosaurus Rex still ramps in all his grisly Southern vigour." Irving Layton he describes as "a ring-tailed roarer in the little zoo of Canadian letters," while Hugh MacLennan's novel *The Watch that Ends the Night* reveals "a suave mawkishness about sex which amounts almost to diplomatic evasion." The anarchists of the 1940s identified themselves with the great assassins "as a hearth cat might imagine himself a lion."

How can an anarchist, who wants to do away with governments and nations altogether, edit a magazine devoted to a national literature? Some of our more adamant nationalists would say flatly that he can't; that Woodcock's international perspective and principled distaste for emotional nationalism make him thoroughly unsuitable for the job. And although there can be no doubt of Woodcock's competence or interest–he has written at least three books on Canadian literature and edited several more–it is true that he maintains an uneasy balance between patriotism and anarchism.

"I really accept Orwell's distinction between nationalism and patriotism," Woodcock argues. "To me, nationalism is the fervid kind of thing that is exclusive, that tries at least by implication to set one's own culture higher than all other cultures, that fears one's own culture will be ruined by the influence of other cultures. But basic in anarchism is a kind of regionalism, and I think I'd call myself a regionalist patriot, in that I'm very attached to the land: it's the place where I live, it's the place where I've managed to work more happily than anywhere else.

"Therefore I have a feeling for it, I have a loyalty towards it, I feel there are certain things that belong to this country or to this region that are not found anywhere else, and that these things should be cultivated. I don't think it's at all incompatible with anarchism to see the world as a pattern of rich cultures all distinct from each other. The anarchists *believe* in a variety of cultures, interacting one on the other. So I don't think there's anything incompatible with editing *Canadian Literature* and holding anarchist ideas. In fact I'd rather like to go on one day and perhaps edit a *Kootenay Literature* or something."

Throughout Woodcock's work, hints of the good society emerge. It would be based on firm local loyalties like Woodcock's own attachment to British Columbia, and on concrete communities of interest: producers' groups, factories run by guilds of workers, villagers, townspeople. These would lead to a loose regional federalism—all the villages in Cape Breton, say, uniting to attack joint problems—and ultimately to an even looser national federation. "Within this structure," Woodcock writes, "the principle to follow would be the minimization of remote control, coupled with the maximization of responsibility through participation. In other words, any decision of any kind that affects only a local group must be reached by that group alone and by consensus if possible." Combined with a wide use of the referendum and the initiative, and with all elected officials subject to immediate recall by their constituents, Woodcock's utopian Canada would be democratic in a way few of us have even dared imagine. But in another sense, it is not so very different from the country we have now: the main change is that the real focus of power becomes very local, where democracy functions best already. For Woodcock, one of the great charms of this country is its complete failure to become a unified, centrally-controlled nation-state like France or England or even the United States. Despite the many ties that bind Canadians, Canada remains balky, stubbornly regional, cross-hatched with barriers of language, geography, religion, economics. Woodcock loves that: in the loose mesh of Canada, people have a chance to breathe.

Woodcock wrote his book on anarchism in 1962 as a kind of dirge for a movement which had passed into the graveyard of history. He was agreeably surprised when the next few years revealed a great revival of its central ideas: extreme freedom and democratic responsibility, decentralization, respect for human variety, non-violence, for, despite the enthusiasm for terrorism of some past anarchists, Woodcock insists anarchism is appropriately non-violent. The pure anarchist society, he admits, is an ideal "which will probably never be realized. But the very presence of such a concept of pure liberty can help us to judge our condition and see our aims."

Anarchism thus becomes "a kind of extreme philosophy which presents one with a goal," Woodcock argues, as the light fades in the east-facing windows of his office. "There is something on the horizon, but you don't necessarily feel that in your lifetime you're going to tramp as far as that horizon. Nevertheless it's something that does condition your relations with people, your attitude towards politics as they exist, your attitude towards the organization of society. And I think you can be anarchist-oriented in your relations with society without necessarily thinking you're going to establish the totally free society."

The anarchist hunches over a desk in Vancouver, his horn-rimmed glasses reflecting the light, his hands rippling over the typewriter. This year he has published a book on Amor de Cosmos, second premier of B.C., and a collection from *Canadian Literature* called *The Canadian Novel in the Twentieth Century.* He is writing a book on Gabriel Dumont, Louis Riel's chief lieutenant, rebel patriot of the French-Canadian West. For the anarchist, the dreams of Dumont may well be plain common sense.

"The great anarchists," George Woodcock has written, "call on us to stand on our own moral feet like a generation of princes, to become aware of justice as an inner fire, and to learn that the still, small voices of our own hearts speak more truly than the choruses of propaganda that daily assault our outer ears.''

The black flag of anarchy flies proudly in Kerrisdale, by George.

(May, 1975)

A Chinese Grocer Named Angus:

His actual name, it appears, is Yat Hang Mew, but everyone knew him as Angus. He is one of those shadowy figures one remembers from childhood with diffuse affection: always present, always smiling, assuring a child by his mere presence that familiar things were in their familiar places. Angus was the proprietor of Varsity Produce, a greengrocer's shop at 10th and Sasamat, in the university district of Vancouver.

Angus, genuinely, has a place among my earliest memories. We moved to Vancouver in 1939, when I was two, to a house at 3rd and Sasamat; after a year or so we moved up to West 23rd, but before we moved Angus had anchored himself firmly in our lives. My mother would lift the phone and give the number, and

A PORTRAIT OF
YAT HANG MEW

when Angus answered she would tell him what she wanted. Then she would ask him whether he had any "unusual commodities," and if he had, say, fresh asparagus she would order that.

An hour or two later Angus would clatter down the street in his truck, an old Dodge pickup the colour of well-laundered blue jeans, with a high canopy like an open carport built up over the box. Up the steps he would come, his box laden with tomatoes and cabbage, apples and asparagus. He'd smile and chat a moment, and then he'd be off again, idling down the street to the next customer.

I somehow thought of him as an old man, but then when you're three or four everyone over ten seems venerable. Those days are now distant and sunlit as a mirage, those days before dial telephones and automatic transmissions, when a young professor and his wife could hire a maid for $17.00 a month and her keep, while they went out to lectures and heard a scientist say that after the war a new miracle material would completely transform our lives. It would probably be known as "plastic."

Years pass, things change, boys grow up. Home delivery became a wistful memory, and we learned to shop by car in supermarkets. Angus, I vaguely realized, was still in business. When I went to college, I drove up 10th Avenue every day, and there was the little wooden shop, with the flowers and fruit and vegetables standing on the sidewalk under the awnings. I stopped in occasionally, and there was Angus, apparently untouched by the passage of twenty years.

I walked off the big jetliner from Montreal in the spring of 1975 into a cloud of immigrants from Asia, Indians mostly, for Vancouver is—as Vancouverites somewhat uneasily boast—Canada's gateway to the Orient. Black skins, brown, white and yellow; turbans, saris, business suits and Pentax cameras; a jangle of languages, and English spoken to the lilts of a dozen other cultures; a rich *pot-pourri* of humanity swirling around my petite, white-haired mother. We drove downtown, and I installed myself on the seventeenth floor of a hotel tower, and Mother said I should look up Angus.

"Angus! Is he still alive?"

"He certainly is," said Mother. "He sold the Varsity Produce several years ago, and now he's in real estate. He's doing very well.

"I'm sure he'd love to see you. Did you know he was at your father's funeral?"

That was in '51, and no, I hadn't known he was there. It says something attractive about Angus that he would trouble to go—and something attractive about my father, too—that he should inspire that farewell.

I found Angus in a spacious yellow stuccoed house on a broad, well-tended lot about a block from the site of his old shop. He met me at the door, dapper in a three-piece suit, a Chinese newspaper in his hand, a cheerful, confident man who has been touched very lightly by the thirty-five summers which have flown since we met. He ushered me into a comfortable living room, settled himself in a chair among the poinsettias, fan palms and philodendrons, inquired about my mother, and told me something of his life.

How little we know of the people around us! What extraordinary quests and trials, what despairs and ecstasies are hidden behind the eyes we meet casually in the bus, at the beach, over the counter! And history: how we are all the playthings of history, of chance and mythology.

Angus was born in Shekki, in the Pearl River district of Kwangtung Province, about eighty miles from Hong Kong. He was one of ten children, and his older brother, Yat Kai Mew, had migrated to Canada. At fifteen, Yat Hang Mew followed him. But his brother, ten years older, couldn't sponsor him; the federal government had just passed an immigration act which had the effect of cutting off Chinese immigration into Canada. Between 1911 and 1922, roughly 2,300 Chinese a year had entered Canada. During the next twenty-three years a grand total of eight were admitted. The only exceptions were merchants, consuls and students; and so it was that Yat Hang Mew entered Canada as a student, the son of Jung Won Leung.

He enrolled in Strathcona School, in a class almost entirely Chinese. "I wanted to learn English, you know?" he grins, speaking half a century later with a touch still of Chinese accent. "So I took the first seat in the first row, right up front. I didn't want to miss *anything*. Our teacher, Miss Coleman, she spoke a little bit of Chinese. Her father was a missionary in China, and he *really* spoke Chinese, but she didn't pronounce it well; it's hard, a hard language. We had a lot of fun with her pronunciation.

"Well, after a couple of weeks she said, 'That's enough fooling around, we have to get down to work. I'm going to put a list of English names on the board, and I want each of you to pick one, then you'll have a name English people can remember.' So she put the list on the blackboard, and I thought, I'm in the first seat in the first row, so I'll take the first name. Which was 'Angus.' The names were all the same to me, you know. But it was a good choice. Wherever I went, people remembered 'Angus.'

"Then I had a choice, which high school to go to. I could have gone to King Ed, where there were lots of our people, but I chose Kitsilano. I was the only Chinese student in the school, and that's why I went. The only way to learn a language is to plunge right in. You have to answer questions, explain yourself–understand everything–all in English."

Angus had a friend, Kee Gee, who ran a farm in Coquitlam, and who hadn't mastered English very well. "He would get advice from the Canadian farmers," Angus remembers, "and he couldn't understand what they were telling him. So I used to interpret for him. Then a bit later he bought the Varsity Produce, and put my name in as his partner, even though I was in China at the time. He's a wonderful man, just a wonderful man; we were partners thirty-seven years and we never had a quarrel–"

Wait a minute, now. You were in *China*?

"Oh yes. We used to go back to China every four or five years." He laughs. "Most people take vacations a couple of weeks a year, but we went for a whole year, and the other partner took care of the shop." He laughs again. "We had a good business, we made lots of money. If I'd invested it all I'd be a millionaire today. But we spent it travelling back and forth to China, you see? We were really working for the CPR."

For twenty-five years, in fact, Angus had two lives. In China he married, acquired property, and fathered three children. In Canada he ran the Varsity Produce, invested what he could, and waited patiently for the immigration laws to be eased. If he had wanted to, Angus would have been hard-pressed to find a Chinese bride in Canada; as James Morton points out in his recent book on the Chinese in B.C., *In the Sea of Sterile Mountains*, the 1941 census showed over 16,000 Chinese men in the province, and only 2,400 women—a result, presumably, of B.C.'s virulent anti-Orientalism. Men might be permitted in to do jobs white men disdained, but we were not about to encourage them to bring their wives and settle.

Morton's book is painful reading. Here is Premier S.F. Tolmie sternly warning that "the country and its representatives had better wake up if we are to preserve Canada as a white man's country." Here is Fred Hume, later Mayor of both New Westminster and Vancouver, seconding a motion in favour of complete exclusion of Oriental immigrants. Here is A.M. Manson, Attorney-General and later a Supreme Court Justice, declaring that "We want B.C. to be a white man's country." Here are women's groups, early socialists, the Board of Trade, the Farmers' Institute and the B.C. Federation of Labour all clamoring against the Chinese.

Worst of all, here is the Asiatic Exclusion League meeting in 1907, being addressed by a Presbyterian minister, the Rev. Dr. H.W. Fraser, who claims that if the influx is not stopped at once, his own pulpit will soon be in the hands of "a Jap or a Chinaman." Thirty thousand people listened to such tripe, spoken from the steps of the City Hall, on the very edge of the Chinese quarter. Not surprisingly, a mob that night rampaged through Chinatown, smashing windows and beating Chinese people while families cowered in their barricaded stores.

That was the year Angus was born. By the time he got to Canada, things were a little better, but as late as 1935, when he was well-established in business, a full-page ad for the Liberal Party said, in part, that "A vote for any CCF candidate is a vote to give the Chinaman and Japanese the same voting right that you have! A vote for a Liberal candidate is a vote against Oriental enfranchisement."

As Angus says, "We were then where the East Indians are today." Even the occupations open to a Chinese were severely limited. "We were good farmers," Angus smiles, "so we were

141

allowed to farm. We were good cooks, so we could operate restaurants. We could run laundries or small food stores, we could work in the lumber mills, just the same way the black people were allowed to be porters and work on the railways. That was all that was allowed."

So Angus and Kee Gee made themselves into the best damn greengrocers you ever saw. At 4.00 or 5.00 in the morning Kee Gee would take the other truck, the big International, down to Chinatown, where the market gardeners from South Vancouver and the Fraser Delta would have the produce stacked in boxes along the curb. "To get something scarce, something unusual, you have to be there early, you see?" explains Angus. I wish I had seen it: the Chinese farmers, the owners of little groceries all over town, the trucks creeping along in the darkness while the boxes were put off and on, the haggling in the singing dialects of China, the greetings, the jokes, the money changing hands. "All gone now," Angus shrugs. "Old fashioned. Now the farmers sell direct to the wholesale departments of the chain stores." In its day, though, the Keefer Street market must have been like Covent Garden conducted in Chinese, in the heart of a city I once considered bland.

"The whole secret of our business was estimating," Angus declares. "We had to estimate exactly how much we'd need of each kind of produce, how much we could sell that day—you know—not to run short, but not to be left with produce that would go bad. Everything we dealt with was perishable: fruit, vegetables, flowers. You had to estimate *exactly*.

"Every day of the year is different. Different things in season, different volume of business—December 24, Christmas Eve—that was the busiest day of the whole year. The shop would be jammed in the morning, and we'd rush, rush all day, and by the evening there wouldn't be a thing left except maybe one bunch of flowers, and sombody would hurry in and say, 'Yes, that's just what I want!'"

In the early days, Kee Gee and some of the employees had trouble remembering the names of their customers, though they could remember the addresses. "I got an extra Point Grey phone book," Angus chuckles. "It wasn't very big then, not that many people had phones. I cut it all up and rearranged it by street and house number, so you could say, 4510 West 7th—okay, that's Mrs. So-and-so. People were really *surprised* that we always knew the names, even if we were only there once." He giggles. "I never told them about that phone book."

Angus insisted that Varsity Produce offer personal service.

"You had to know that with this person the back door is open, and you're supposed to go in, put the vegetables in the ice box, the fruit in the bowl on the table, and she'll leave a vase out for the flowers. Or if a lady comes along and says she's having a party Saturday night and she wants to serve avocados, then I know I have to get them Tuesday and ripen them in the warm room; not too fast, or I'll cook them and they'll be like rubber. You see? You can buy them green, but you can't serve them that way, they're worth nothing."

Half-way across the world, the armies of Japan were marching into China. Angus' wife tried to protect the three children, tried to ensure they were fed and sheltered, even if it meant becoming rundown and undernourished herself. Eventually she contracted tuberculosis, and when Canada's immigration laws were finally relaxed in 1947 to permit the entry of wives and unmarried children, Ng Wai Leung was still barred by her health. She died in 1952, and Angus brought the children to Vancouver.

A light suddenly broke over me.

"Angus," I said, "when I was in high school a fellow named Jock Leung came into our class in the middle of the year. He was straight from China, and he could hardly speak any English at all—"

"Jock, yes," grinned Angus. "My oldest son." He points to a framed graduation portrait. "That's him there, he's a doctor now."

Imagine that: I remember it vividly, this kid a bit older than the rest of us, and everyone wanting to be friendly and make him feel at home, but stymied and embarrassed by the language gap. I remember we smiled a lot, and he smiled back, and gradually, over the years, he learned our language and—Angus' son.

"Bright guy," I said, studying the picture for some trace of the shy, friendly boy who joined our class all those years ago.

"He gets that from his mother," Angus nodded. "No, really he does. When I went back to China, I used to spend my time studying Chinese language and literature. I remember my wife saying, 'Come to bed! It's late!' and I would say, 'No, I have to repeat this essay for my teacher tomorrow–that's the way they taught, you see, you had to memorize a whole essay at a time.'

"Well, you're pretty dumb if you can't do *that*, said my wife, and she repeated the whole thing off, lying there in bed. *I* hadn't learned it, but *she'd* learned the whole essay just from hearing me repeat it over and over. Jock has that from her. So has my daughter Florence, in the other picture, she's a nurse. My second son, Norman, he's dead."

"I'm sorry, Angus."

Angus was silent for a little while.

In 1956 Angus went back to Hong Kong and married his second wife, Anne. They have four children, three girls and a boy, and the youngest, Winston, is the same age as my eldest. Which says something amusing about my assumption, years ago, that Angus was an old man. He's only sixty-seven now, in fact.

How did he get into real estate?

"I told you about my partner, what a fine man he is, and how he trusted me. Oh, he trusted me! And I trusted him, too. In the evening he would tell me what he paid at the market in the morning, and I would give it to him–never questioned–never questioned! And he didn't question me. If I had to go downtown and I was a long time getting back, he never said, 'Where were you, we needed you at the shop'–because he *knew* if I stayed downtown there was a good reason. I was the privileged one, you know, I dealt with the customers, did all the banking, all the paying, kept the books, and I didn't go downtown at 4.00 in the morning, either! At the end of the year, I would give him a paper, saying This is what we took in, this is what we spent, here's the profit, and here's your half–and I'd give him the money.

"But he'd take the paper, and he'd do this!" Angus crumples up a sheet of paper. "And he'd throw it in the stove! I'd say, Hey, don't *do* that, I can't get you another. But he said, 'I got my money, what do I need a paper for?'

"Well, we had a customer on 10th, just where the Bank of

Montreal is now, a very nice lady. I used to take her groceries over and sometimes I'd have a cup of coffee with her and talk for a few minutes at the end of the day. I'd be gone from the shop, but my partner would never say anything about it. One night, I was just coming from her place and I saw a For Sale sign going up on a building across the street. We'd been looking for some property to invest in but we couldn't find anything. So we bought that one, and that was the beginning of it."

Now Angus owns, he says, "a few pieces of property." Rumour has it that he actually owns several considerable pieces of income property in the premium shopping area just outside the university gates. The housewives who once bought their groceries from him are getting on in years now, and some of them are moving into apartments; I know of one, at least, who has found herself doing business with Angus once again.

By the mid-sixties, things had changed. Where Angus once lived above the shop, sending money to his family in China, he now lived with his second family in the big house round the corner. The Chinese community not only had the vote, but had even sent a member to Parliament. Chinese-Canadians were prominent in medicine, dentistry, and the law; no longer hived up in Chinatown, Chinese families were spread throughout the city.

"Everything changed after the war," Angus believes. "A lot of our people fought with the Canadian forces, and when they came home they wanted to be treated like anyone else. When we go into battle we're all the same, so how come we can't live in the same districts?"

People like Angus, however, remained in an oddly precarious position. Well-established though they might be, they were still illegal immigrants, subject to deportation. One of the darker results was blackmail. "When someone found out your name was not what you said it was," Angus remarks, "they would threaten you: pay me so much or I turn you in. Lots of people paid, but I didn't. I said, I'd rather go back to China, and have *you* in jail for extortion. I don't like to be pushed around. Well, that man dropped the whole thing."

Ultimately the federal government offered illegal immigrants a

145

chance to normalize their status, and, after some hesitation, Angus did so. "The immigration officer was suspicious," he recalls. "He said, 'Why did you take so long? Who are you protecting?' Well, of course, I wasn't protecting anyone; the person who arranged the papers for me to come to Canada was dead by then, but I told him I had a business as Angus Leung, and children to think about—Jock, pharmacies and everyone knew him as Dr. Leung, and it wasn't easy to go back to my true name. Actually Jock didn't change. But when I told the immigration man all that, then he understood."

Angus was thinking about giving up his business, too.

"The way we did business is outa date, outa date. You can get anything in Safeway now. When we started you couldn't, but now you can. The bank had been after our property for years, and West Point Grey is growing so fast, a little grocery store can't stand in the way of progress. And my children were in school, but I never saw them, I was in the shop till 10.00, 10.30 at night. My wife said, Angus, they need you; I can't speak enough English to help them with their schoolwork."

In 1968, Angus sold the Varsity Produce. He had been doing business at 10th and Sasamat for thirty-seven years. He thought he had retired; but then his friends began asking him for advice about real estate. He had good connections in the Chinese community, he was known as a shrewd investor, and before long he had a realtor's license and an arrangement with Sasamat Realty. Last year he more or less became inactive, though he still makes a deal or two when one comes along. Now he devotes his time to his family, his friends, his fellows in the West Point Grey United Church.

"Westerners," he says, "are ahead of the Chinese in technology, no question about that. But we are way ahead in family life, in friendship. And those things matter too."

Nobody who surveys the wreckage of modern Canadian family life can possibly deny it. There is something to be learned from Angus, from his cheerful perseverance in the face of prejudice and restriction, from the balance with which his living room remains Canadian, and yet is subtly transformed by the artistry and values of a civilization which was old when Socrates began teaching in the little town of Athens.

Vancouver as a whole is perhaps beginning to achieve a little of that balance. Anyone can see the relationship between Montreal and Paris, between Halifax and London; the flavour of Vancouver, by contrast, is considerably Asian, from the restaurants and import shops to the Nitobe Gardens and the Asian Studies program at UBC, from the Sikh temples to the Japanese officers of the fishermen's union, from the Roberts Bank superport which ships coal to Japan to the little groceries across the city which, like the Varsity Produce, are invariably run by the Chinese.

"Racial discrimination," declared Alan Morley in *Vancouver. From Milltown to Metropolis* (1969) "is a thing of the past in Vancouver." At the time it must have seemed so; today, with the influx from Hong Kong and India over the past few years, racism is again rearing its distorted features in the city. It is hardly surprising: with a vacancy rate of less than 1 per cent in housing and elementary school classes in which only three children of forty speak English, the city's systems are under considerable strain. "In another generation," a Vancouverite muttered to me ominously, "our children are going to be working for these people." Perhaps. And why not? If you have to have a boss, what difference does it make that his skin is yellow, or brown, or candy-striped? If I had to work again for wages, I would be grateful for an employer of Angus' wit, cheerfulness and humanity.

Canadians are debating immigration policy these days with a vigour we have not seen for years, and immigration is a long-term investment. It hurts at the time, and the benefits flow only in the distant future. But we could do worse than to remember Angus, the corner grocer who carved such a niche for himself in the life of West Point Grey, who nourished our avocados while his family waited patiently in China. We did our best to keep him out. If we had succeeded, we would have been much the poorer.

(April, 1975)

147

From Vienna to the Potlatch, With Love:

In the rain forest of Vancouver Island, the Indians are singing. Six or eight drummers sit in a semi-circle, and the singers, Frank Williams and some women, dance gracefully, taking small steps. They float, says an Indian, explaining their style. The women dancers show the rhythm, the man provides the excitement.

This is a Quinquatla dance, a social dance which can deal with any theme. This particular Quinquatla is a victory dance. Victory, notes George Clutesi, the Nootka artist and author, doesn't have to do with wars alone. It is more "the victory of one's own fears, weaknesses, foibles, jealousies and the dread of want."

The drums beat steadily. The dancers float. In the background of this large field in Port Alberni, dogs bark and children play.

A PORTRAIT OF

IDA HALPERN

And a woman, a white woman, manipulates a primitive disc recorder connected to its power source by yards of umbilical extension cord. She knows nothing about recording, but she senses the drums will be too loud. She strains to raise the microphone nearer the singers, further from the insistent drums.

The year is 1951, and Ida Halpern is the only white person in attendance. Frank Williams died shortly after, but you can hear the song on Dr. Halpern's 1974 Folkways album *Nootka: Indian Music of the Pacific North West Coast.*

Ida Halpern may travel on to adjudicate a music festival in Nanaimo or Victoria. Then she will go back to her house on West 37th Avenue in Vancouver to work on a broadcast for the CBC, the BBC, the radio network of Germany or Austria. She will go out for an evening of bridge with her husband, Dr. George Halpern. And she will give piano lessons to a few privileged children.

We didn't know we were privileged, of course. Children never do.

Every Tuesday afternoon at 4.00, characteristically a bit late for my lesson, I would fly down the Dunbar hill on my cranky old CCM bicycle, a rain cape over my shoulders, water streaming from my hair, my sheet music carefully zipped into its flat leather case in the carrier. I would make my way into the dark, exotic-smelling house, and Regina Victoria, the frisky Irish setter, would bound all over me.

"Reggie! *Reggie!*" Ida Halpern would say. "So, Donald. You are wet. Let me take zat."

And we would go to the grand piano which filled what was meant for a dining room. I would play my scales and *etudes,* insufficiently practised over the week-end, and Ida Halpern would nod her head quizzically.

"You have expression, yes?" she would say. "But you are careless. We try it again. So. *One* and two and *sree* and four..."

As George Bernard Shaw pointed out, youth is a wonderful thing: it's a shame to see it wasted on kids. I learned a great deal from Ida Halpern. To this day there is a piano in my living room, on which I periodically hammer out my frustrations and delights. But I didn't learn a tenth of what I might have.

I didn't grasp, for instance, that Dr. Halpern was the first musicologist in Canada, with all the rich cultural background implied by a doctorate from the University of Vienna. It never occurred to me that Hitler's *Anschluss*, the annexation of Austria by Germany in 1938, might have something to do with their arrival in Vancouver. I knew, vaguely, that my piano teacher was interested in Indian music; but in those days the Indians were simply regarded as drunken, lazy and primitive. An interest in native music was a curious eccentricity, nothing more. Certainly it never occurred to me that she might be doing something of great cultural importance to her adopted country.

No. I remember George Halpern, his hands reddening in my mother's scalding dishwater, protesting that "Zis water is too hot, Hazel! It is not necessary!" He may have been a famous pharmaceutical chemist, but Mother was a Prairie Scot: the water stayed hot. I remember Ida showing me the latest litter produced by her cat, who bred offspring as though she reckoned her species were endangered. I remember George, who has always looked like a stout, balding cherub, expostulating to my father that "In Austria, we drank for ze pleasure of drinking. In Canada, one drinks to get *dronk*!" And that, said my father to me, is a sensible observation, the kind of attitude which might govern an intelligent man's approach to liquor.

I never knew that when Ida Halpern arrived at the Canadian Immigration offices in Vancouver in 1939 and was asked what she would do in Canada, she replied that she would collect Indian music. "Ze immigration officer just laughed and said, 'Well, you will have to think of something better that that.' You know, there was a great distrust, and people just looked down at it. Zey couldn't believe that the dirty Indian has a music. It is changed now completely, but then people couldn't have any appreciation that the Indian has a culture."

And the Indians were equally uneasy. Accustomed to contempt, they viewed with suspicion this strange woman who seemed actually interested in them and their music. "Music," explains Ida, "is very sacred for them, and it is a form of wealth too." She spent six years making contacts, talking with Kwakiutl and Nootka, Salish and Haida, before she collected so much as a single song. The younger Indians didn't know the songs and didn't care about them; the older people, who did know them, were shocked at the idea of sharing them.

"Every person owns a song," Ida explains, "and ze song is a purely individual thing. It belongs to that person, and nobody else is allowed to sing it. Ze songs–they get them in visions–or they buy them from the songmaker, who makes them just for that certain person. That person can give it by inheritance to his children, but by very strict sociological rules: ze father gives it to the son and to the nephew; ze mother gives her songs to the daughter. If a chief marries a woman, she brings him as dowry her songs. Some songs which come as a dowry are only allowed to be sung after one year, after the first child comes, or something.

"The more songs a person owned, the greater prestige he had. Ze songs were all–for instance the totem poles–for every bird, or every emblem on them, there is a song. Everything has a song, for the Indians. It's fantastic. If you think how many songs could you sing, or I, or–they knew a hundred songs, like that." She snaps her fingers. "Now Mungo Martin, you know Mungo Martin?" Of course I do, the great Kwakiutl carver who before his death in 1963 carved the towering poles in the University of British Columbia's Totem Park, the man behind the Kwakiutl house in Victoria's Thunderbird Park. "He gave me over a hundred songs, hundred thirty, something like that. He sung a whole year for me, while he was working in Vancouver."

Mungo Martin, in fact, was reproached by other chiefs for having given away his songs. "I was a sick man when starting to sing for her," Martin replied. "Now after the year's singing I sang myself to health and am well again."

"Ze younger people were not interested," Ida remarks, thinking back on those early years. "They wanted to be Westernized, they were not proud of their culture. It's–it's how younger people look down on older people, you know? I didn't get a song until Chief Billy Assu–he was a very mighty chief and a very clever man. He had three very handsome sons, good fishermen and so, and none of them knew their songs. Billy Assu was a songmaker too, and I said, Chief, what will happen to your songs if you die? *'They die with me.'* You see, I got across to him that that's what I would like, to keep the culture alive. Ze minute he understood, he said, *'You come: I give you hundred songs.'* I went to the reserve and I stayed with them ten days, and I couldn't stay longer; he gave me eighty-eight songs. And he would have made the hundred. That was the first breakthrough."

When Ida Halpern talks of Billy Assu, Mungo Martin and her other Indian informants, it's easy to see how she succeeded in collecting the songs no white person had ever heard: she quite obviously admires the culture of the Indians and cares particularly deeply for their music; above all, she respects and cares for them as people. When she speaks of Billy Assu, her voice grows tender, and no wonder. Billy Assu was born in 1867, and in his youth the Kwakiutl still mounted slaving raids along the coast. He was chosen and trained to lead his people into the new, white-dominated age, and while he fully understood the lore of his people he was equally capable of dealing with whites. Under his leadership, his village of Cape Mudge was rebuilt, a school was established and a teacher found, liquor sellers were kept out, and the Kwakiutl found jobs in canneries and logging camps, making perhaps as smooth a transition to modern life as any Indian community anywhere. He lived nearly a century, and by the time of his death had not only been decorated by George VI and Elizabeth II, but had retained his hold on the affections of his people.

"He told me he held on to his ceremonial costume even when threatened with prison," Ida Halpern has written, "and he was most unhappy that potlatches were forbidden. In his wisdom, he said, 'There would not be any harm to let them continue. Gradually they will die anyway.'" The potlatch, of course, was the central institution in Coast Indian culture, the climax of cultural and social life, a great feast and gift-giving occasion through which a chief–or anyone else–might establish his prestige by giving away everything but his house, and entertaining hundreds of guests for up to six months. In return, he might expect to receive even more extravagant gifts at subsequent potlatches. Billy Assu himself gave several hundred potlatches, the most famous being the one in celebration of his Big House, three hundred feet long by a hundred feet wide and fifty feet high. The house was packed with food and gifts, including many gold and silver bracelets and 6,000 blankets. Sixteen tribes sent over 3,000 people, and the celebration went on for three weeks.

Many of the songs are associated with potlatches, which involved music at every turn. Ceremonial singing accompanied the visiting chiefs as each was led by the host to his appointed place; dances and songs mingled with speeches and orations. The banning of the potlatch from 1851 to 1954 must surely rank as one of the most pointlessly cruel impositions in the whole sorry litany of white treatment of Indians.

> You go ahead
> And have a good time all over the world
> Chief all over the world
> Shouting out
> Wonderful way I stand
> Chief over all the world

It is a potlatch song of Billy Assu, a marvellously proud, exultant verse: a far cry from Vienna.

Heinrich Ruhdoerfer was active in the silk industry, his wife Sabine was an amateur pianist, and his daughter Ida was "*l'enfant prodige*," she smiles, a child prodigy. "I was ze only child, spoiled, but it didn't hurt me." At the age of nine she gave an all-Beethoven piano concert, "but then," she says, "my parents had the good sense to give me a right childhood, you know? Because if I would have had to develop into a childhood of a pianist, then there wouldn't be any childhood. They wanted me to have a solid education. I am grateful, very grateful; I think the life of a concert pianist or a concert musician is a rotten one. They pay for their gifts terrifically. They *give* a lot, but it makes them quite unhappy people. They have no childhood, zat is gone, but later on in life if they are married they are always separated from their husband or wife and family, they travel—and nerves, and constant exacting practice, because if you don't practise the whole time you are in trouble."

She went to a private school, gave one concert a year, and moved on to the University of Vienna to study musicology—the history and structure of music—and physics, "which go nicely together."

Did she meet George at the university? "No," she declares, with a coquettish sidelong glance, "George is much older zan I. George had his Ph.D. already ten years before I had mine. He was already very well-known when I was in hospital; I heard his name mentioned because he developed the first diuretic pill. That was just like a phenomenon, because it took so much water out of people. It went all over the world. He worked it out with ze medical profession, and when I was in hospital I heard everywhere about that pink pill, about Dr. Halpern, Dr. Halpern, Dr. George Halpern! That was about three years before I met him."

They were married in 1936. There were never any children, which is a pity: they both enjoy young people, they would have made spectacular parents. Even now, when Ida's ex-students come home from California, from eastern Canada or elsewhere, they often seek her out. In 1938, Austria disappeared behind the borders of a militant Nazi Germany. After six anxious months Ida got her Ph.D. and the Halperns left their native country for good.

"George's sister was a very gifted person, she was a professor of neurology and psychiatry and she was called to China to establish ze first chair in those fields in 1931. So we went to Shanghai, and of course she taught at four universities, and they were delighted to have a musicologist from Vienna, so I right away got a position as lecturer at Shanghai University. It was an interesting experience. Ze social life was so terrific: evenings always only evening gowns, and I had all my relations still back in Austria, I didn't feel like celebrating every night." George's father was a Surgeon-General in the army, and eventually died a natural death; Ida's parents did not survive the war.

"I got acquainted with Chinese music, and I made some research in Chinese music, of course. You see, what is now called ethnomusicology is really a part of musicology. Comparative musicology it was called before, but now comparative musicology took such a great dimension because interest in native songs, yes? is so tremendous and so much research is done that a whole science has started itself. That is ethnomusicology. As I came to China, of course, I was fascinated with Chinese music, and I started to like it very much. One transcription of it I learned – there are so many transcriptions of it – but one system I learned.

154

And of course all my students were Chinese."

What language did she teach in?

"English!" she cries, with a deep laugh. "And I must tell you zat ze students understood me better than ze English and American teachers–because I wasn't so idiomatic, of course, I didn't speak so well, not so fast, halting–much more to their taste."

But by the end of a year, the Japanese were advancing in China. Shanghai was surrounded, and everyone wanted out. "A lovely Scotchman, Mr. Murray, bless him" was head of the Canadian chartered banks in the Far East, and he asked the Halperns if they had ever thought of going to Canada. They were interested, and when he came home on sabbatical, Murray arranged it.

"We came on the last Empress of Asia boat," Ida recalls. "Ze next one was already the war. I nearly wanted to wait for the next boat, because the next boat would have stayed anchored in Hawaii, and I wanted to see Hawaii, but then I thought, No, let's get out of China–so we went–thank Heavens, because we wouldn't have made it otherwise."

They were heading for Toronto, with its Conservatory, but "we fell in love with Vancouver, with the mountains and the sea–and ze *people*–ze people were just lovely to us." The President of the University of Shanghai had given her a letter to President Klinck of UBC, and "Klinck was charming, he opened all the doors. I have never regretted; and then in the east you don't have the Indian music any more, it is already so watered down, so assimilated."

She taught the first music courses at the university in 1940, and taught in the Summer Session for over twenty years. The director of the Summer Session happened to be my father, and through their friendship my own musical education, spotty though it is, was begun. Meanwhile Ida was writing musical criticism for the daily *Province*, sending reports to the *Musical Courier* of New York, founding the Friends of Chamber Music (irreverently dubbed "the Potty Pals") who brought outstanding chamber groups to Vancouver, adjudicating festivals and judging at auditions for the Metropolitan Opera. She did a CBC series in French, which she has known since childhood. "In French," she laughs, "I have no accent. But in English–!" She also knows

Latin, Italian and Spanish as well as her native German.

She should have been on the university faculty, but there was no music department when she came, and when one was established the anti-feminine bias of the university, which even now complicates and distorts the professional development of gifted women, was virulent enough to keep her out. The odd result is that Ida's life during those years looks like a professor's life except that she held no university job. She published papers, attended scholarly conferences, contributed to museum projects and encyclopaedias. And at every opportunity, she carried on her research on the music of the Indians.

"I suppose maybe zat is a European hangover," she muses, "that you do research for the research sake, and not for money. You know? On this continent–it is good, it is wise–research is paid. In Europe not. You make research on your own."

In 1956, the brand-new university in Burnaby, Simon Fraser, made her a founding member of its Convocation and an Honorary Associate of its Centre for Communications and the Arts. She attended a folk music conference in Ghana in 1966, and the next year arranged for the world-famous scholars she met there to attend a workshop in Vancouver; the *Proceedings* of that workshop are now in their third printing, a well-known text on ethnomusicology. That same year the first of her records, *Indian Music of the Pacific Northwest Coast*, was issued by Folkways; in 1974 it was followed by a second collection, *Nootka*. Each set contains two long-playing discs and extensive booklets (thirty-six and sixteen pages respectively) about the singers, their culture and their music. The fifty-nine songs included are only a fraction of what Ida Halpern's collection now entails.

We sit in the bright, comfortable house on the brow of Point Grey, where they moved from West 37th, looking over the Jericho flats to the outer harbour and the white spiky towers of downtown. George prospered, establishing his own company, G.R. Chemicals, and the Halperns can afford to live comfortably, can afford, I suddenly notice, an impressive collection of Canadian art to hang in the living room, Lawren Harrises and Emily Carrs, paintings of Indian villages and surging mountains. "Yes," Ida smiles, "This is our Canadian room. Every painting here is Canadian, except that one Chagall. Of course they weren't so expensive when we bought them as they would be now."

George comes in, beaming and joking, ready to wheel in a tea-wagon with pastries and coffee. He has been in hospital, seriously ill; the first day home he walked the beaches in a storm, and today Ida has been chiding him for wearing only a coat and no jacket, for walking outside in his slippers. George grins sheepishly, like a naughty but unrepentant boy. Ida herself is not all that well; she has a heart condition and high blood pressure, and George's illness made them worse. "When George was sick," she has told me, "I couldn't sleep; I came in here and played ze piano, played and played because you don't want to talk how you feel, and anyway who is to talk to at 3.00 in the morning?"

"Coffee, tea, or meelk?" George inquires, miming a stewardess.

For me, Ida Halpern has always been a rich, dynamic, sensual woman, an intellectual who nevertheless gloried in the vitality of her emotional life. I always thought her one of the most warm and desirable women I knew, and at sixty-five she is so still. Fussing over one another, joking and teasing, she and George seem still to be overwhelmed with their good fortune in finding one another; they have grown together, says Ida, characteristically discussing ardour with a scholarly reference to mythology, "like Baucis and Philemon," the aging lovers whose hospitality to the disguised Zeus gave them the gift of dying at the same time and being transformed into an oak and a lime tree. I can imagine Ida, anguished and alone, sweeping into the room in the darkest hours, making the lacquered grand piano tell her devotion and her fear to a sleeping world.

I remember the fire of her playing when she would show me how a piece should go: it was the best part of the music lesson, with her long soft fingers dancing over the keys, the blood-red nails clattering out their own rhythm. And that, perhaps, is what she taught best: the *feeling* for music, the understanding that the scales and the technique and the funny little marks on the page were only a means to an end, and the end was passion and humour and terror, the whole range of human emotion and experience.

And so, though I do not understand the music of the Kwakiutl and the Nootka, I think I understand something of what it means

157

to Ida Halpern. To find an unstudied music, a music new to scholarship, and to find a people who interpreted the world through music, a people who regarded music as wealth, vision and religion–such a discovery bridges the distance from Vienna to Cape Mudge in a single flash. Music, says the old truism, is the universal language.

"Music never lies," says Ida, "it is the truest sign of a culture." Where did the West Coast Indians come from? Were they Asians, crossing to North America by the vanished land-bridge over the Bering Sea? The music, Ida says, may tell us. "I always felt it was not Chinese," she declares and recent scholarship has noted parallels with the music of Polynesia and that of the Ainus, the white pre-Japanese inhabitants of Japan. Ida herself points out that the scale the Indians use is like the ancient scales of Java.

Meanwhile the music which nearly died lives on. A new generation of Indians, proud of their culture and identity, is learning the songs; Ida's collection provides music for plays like Lister Sinclair's *The World of the Wonderful Dark* and for the Encyclopaedia Britannica film *The Legend of the Magic Knives*. Like the notes on the page, Ida Halpern has been the means of making the music part of the heritage not only of the Indians who own it, but of all of us who live in what was once their country only.

I told her she had done a great work for her new country, and she said she hoped so. And that reminded her of something she hadn't thought about for years, the trip to Canada on the Empress of Asia.

"They showed films, yes? And before each one everybody got up and sang God Save Ze Queen–no, ze King–of course. And I thought, how wonderful to be able to sing that, because I didn't have a country, you see? Austria was gone, part of Germany. Canada gave me what I needed most, to–well–to be alive, you know?

"And then I had a country again. And so I say, Thank you. To Canada."

(October, 1975)

158

Home are the Sailors:

The woman wanted $20.00 for the Siamese kitten, but Beryl Smeeton got it for half-price. "You see," explained the breeder, "it's going to have such an *interesting* life."

Indeed it did. Before her death nearly twenty years later, Pwe, as the kitten came to be called, had circled the world in a small boat, terrified a Micronesian maiden on a remote Pacific island, explored the sewers of Paris and the waterfronts of Australia, made her peace with animals ranging from moose to a succession of dogs, caught bats and flying fish in mid-ocean, been twice shipwrecked and had rounded Cape Horn under sail.

She had also embarrassed Beryl's husband, Miles Smeeton. Miles is a six-foot-six former British Army Brigadier, holder of a

A PORTRAIT OF

MYLES & BERYL SMEETON

Military Cross from North Africa and a Distinguished Service Order from the Burmese campaign, an accomplished mountaineer and polo player. He hates to call for help.

One night, anchored during a gale of wind in Hawaii, the Smeetons, their daughter Clio and a friend, John Guzzwell, were playing cards. Miles stepped on deck to use Nature's largest urinal, and heard a plaintive "Maaaoo!" from the water near the bow of the yacht. "I just had time to see Pwe vanishing in the water," he recalls, "so I jumped over and I got her and held her up in the air. I hung onto the anchor chain, and shouted, AHOY! I could hear laughter from inside. So then I thought I'd better drift down to a porthole in the toilet, and I shouted, AHOY! again. More laughter from down below: they were having a good time. So in the end I had to say it, you know, *Hellllppp!*"

"Even then," Beryl laughs, "John said, '*That* chap's nearly had it!'"

Guzzwell was a remarkable young man, who had built the twenty-foot yawl *Trekka* himself behind a fish and chip shop in Victoria, B.C., and who would ultimately bring her home *via* Australia, South Africa and Panama–the smallest ship ever to circumnavigate the world, sailed by the first Englishman ever to do so single-handed. Clio Smeeton was fourteen, and her parents felt she needed a year in an English school. They planned to sail to Melbourne for the 1956 Olympic Games, then send her to England by plane while they followed in their forty-six-foot ketch *Tzu Hang.* The question was, what route would they take? If they sailed south of Australia they would have strong prevailing winds dead on the nose; if they went east and north over the tropical top of the island continent, they would have 1,200 miles of tricky sailing along the Great Barrier Reef.

"Of course," said Beryl, "I would like to go by Cape Horn."

"What!" cried Miles and John. *Cape Horn!*

Below 40 degrees South latitude, the westerly gales blow continuously, almost uninterrupted by land. These are the "Roaring Forties," where the great grain clippers once flew in their hundreds, driving below South America, making three round trips to England in two years. These are the most uncompromising of all the seas and all their power concentrates at Cape Horn, where the ocean bottom rises and the shores of Antarctica and South America reach towards one another across the tumbling wasteland of Drake Passage.

From Australia to the Horn: one of the great sea passages of history, it lies now virtually deserted, rendered obsolete by steam and the Panama Canal. But to sail there is to sail in the track of Drake, Magellan, Cook; its history and its difficulty make a Cape Horn passage still the Mount Everest of sailing. In 1956, the Horn had been rounded by only five yachts: of these one had been lost and another twice rolled over. Even the father of ocean cruising, the great Nova Scotian seaman Joshua Slocum, had taken the inside route through the Straits of Magellan.

"I'd jump at the chance to go with you," said Guzzwell.

Tzu Hang sailed from Melbourne two days before Christmas, 1956, bound for Port Stanley in the Falkland Islands, 6,600 miles away. The voyage would become one of the epic adventures of our time.

On a low table in the barn-like house in Cochrane, Alberta, sealed in plastic, stands a first-day cover of a postage stamp of Tenzing, the Sherpa who accompanied Sir Edmund Hillary to the peak of Mount Everest. Tenzing's autograph makes the envelope practically unique.

"Tenzing," declared Miles, "is one of the few men I've known that just radiated an aura of *goodness*. He was over forty, you know, when he began all this high-powered climbing. It's been very hard for him to adjust to his celebrity since the assault on Everest."

Well, yes, the Smeetons have been friends of Tenzing for the best part of forty years, since before they were married. Their idea of courting was to climb mountains, like the Himalayan peak Tirich Mir, for instance, on which Beryl climbed higher than any woman up to that time. They had four Sherpa porters: Tenzing was among them, and it was one of his earliest climbs. Miles and "Bea," as she's known to her friends, were so taken with Tenzing that they recommended him to other climbers, and eventually he built up such a reputation that when Hillary came along...Oh, yes, he's visited in Cochrane....

161

"We had a great trek in the Himalayas looking for old passes, before we were married," Miles grins. "Great fun. Looking for passes that were no longer known as passes. We did find two or three over the main Hindu Kush range. You could recognize them as passes because there was always the remains of a cairn, but they'd fallen into disuse. Something more fascinating about finding a pass than climbing a mountain. You're sort of looking for it up various glaciers and things like that, you know, climbing ridges, and then suddenly you find it, and the whole country drops away on the other side. Great fun."

Miles' notion of great fun tends to be strenuous; Bea's is even more so, if that's possible. Take the time Miles was going home from India, for instance. Bea was married to someone else, and though neither of them talks much about it, one senses a distant flash of turmoil in the officer's mess, a love story out of Thackeray or C.S. Forester. "Life with her has been one of laughter, and sometimes I wonder how she could have put up with me for so long, and I marvel at the luck that has led me to her," wrote Miles, decades later, though he admitted that "there have been rare occasions when I have felt just the opposite."

"How will you go home?" Bea asked, long ago, in that indistinct British India where cavalry officers like Miles Smeeton held down the outposts of empire.

"Oh, third-class P&O liner, I suppose," replied Miles.

This struck Bea as unspeakably dull, and she persuaded him that the overland route would be much more interesting. Together they planned it: the creeping trains, the lorry from Baghdad to Jerusalem, Istanbul, Greece—"and, in the event," Miles chuckles—"she came with me." Somehow he gives the impression that even now he suspects she came as much for the adventure as for him.

She had, after all, travelled alone through Russia and China, driven across the United States and ridden across the Andes from one isolated farm to another. She had approached the *Times* of London, looking for support. "They didn't give me any money," she laughs, "but they gave me a letter and told me, you know, if you run into a revolution or something you might send us a report. Actually I *did* find myself in a revolution, in Brazil, but I

162

didn't realize it. Revolutions are like that. I've been through two, in Brazil and Portugal, and in both of them you'd never have noticed that this was the real thing."

Miles had met her in 1930, while he was in the Yorkshire Regiment, and he remembers her years of travel as frustrating: he wanted to spend his time with her, and she kept moving around. He served in Jamaica, Egypt and Shanghai before transferring to the Indian Cavalry in 1936, "betrayed" he says, "by a love of horses." They were married in 1938. When the war broke out they were climbing in the Alps. Duty beckoned, Miles opined, stiffening his upper lip. Don't be silly, argued Bea. "If you go back now they'll only send you back to India. And we're having such fun."

Miles served two years in North Africa; Bea, who is half-Australian, took the baby, Clio, and went to Australia. Then Miles was posted to a tank regiment in India, and took it into Burma. Ultimately he commanded an infantry brigade. Meanwhile Beryl had returned to India.

"Bea couldn't stand my being in Burma and having all the excitement of the war, while she was stuck in India. So she put Clio in an infant school and got a job with a very small and select corps which was called the Women's Auxiliary Service, Burma, a canteen force. I didn't know she'd got this job; and I was in Meiktila, where we were completely surrounded. We'd captured the Japanese main base in a rather fine cavalry action, and they had reacted very strongly: they drove up from the south and came back from the north. The only planes that could get in and out were Piper Cubs, which were flying out the seriously wounded and acting as artillery spotters. And this young artillery officer came up to me and said, 'I've just seen your wife at Monywa.' No, you haven't, I said. But he had.

"I'd just been wounded–not badly, only enough to stop fighting for a short time–and he said, 'I can fly you out to Monywa and bring you back the next day.' So I flew out. You could see all the surrounding Japanese, artillery and all that. I saw Bea in Monywa, and then the next day I had to fly back and submit to being besieged again. Great fun. Tremendous fun."

They had bought property on Saltspring Island, B.C., sight unseen; when the war ended, they took up subsistence farming there. But they had assets in England, frozen by the postwar austerity. In 1950 they hit upon the scheme of using their frozen money to buy a boat in England, then sailing it to Canada and selling it. After a search through England and Scotland, they found *Tzu Hang* in Dover. She cost twice as much as they intended to pay; instead of selling her to support the farm, they eventually sold the farm and went sailing.

She was a double-ended ketch, forty-six-feet long, built entirely of teak in Hong Kong in 1938, and she captured the Smeetons' affections at once. "The union was a mystical one," Miles later wrote. "Two people groping in the dark had laid their hands on something that they knew, without knowledge, was good." They had never sailed anything larger than a dinghy, and that only occasionally; nevertheless, after a trial cruise to Holland with an experienced friend, the three Smeetons set off for British Columbia.

Navigation? "Beryl got herself a small sextant, designed for use in lifeboats, and with this and Mary Blewitt's *Celestial Navigation for Yachtsmen*, she was soon able to take and work out a sight. She never really knew what she was doing, nor ever has, but like some fair witch she followed Mary Blewitt's formula, stirred her pot, and out came the right answer." Seamanship? Two days out they were "lying in wet clothes on wet bunks, and wondering whether we were experiencing a gale or not." They were. Learning as they went, they called in Spain, Portugal and the Canary Islands before taking the trade winds across the Atlantic to the West Indies. They cruised the Caribbean, passed through the Panama Canal, visited the Galapagos Islands and turned north. Sixty-three days later they dropped anchor in Esquimalt, just outside Victoria. It was just two weeks short of a year since they had left England.

Three years later, shorn of their farm, they sailed for San Francisco, where they met Guzzwell. The two vessels cruised in company to New Zealand, where Guzzwell laid up his tiny ship in a friend's garage. Then Melbourne, the Olympics, and Cape Horn.

For seven weeks they sailed east, across the Tasman Sea and south of New Zealand, into the Southern Ocean. Through blustery winds and calms, *Tzu Hang* made her hundred miles a day. Pwe played hide and seek, scowled at porpoises, sunned herself when the weather permitted. John took movies and did some carpentry; Miles caught up on his reading, Beryl worked at a sweater for John. Navigation, meals, watches on deck: the routine of a small ship was interrupted only occasionally by a minor emergency; a fitting that broke, a fast sail change. They were 5,000 miles from Australia, with 1,000 miles still between *Tzu Hang* and Cape Horn, when the world's most lonely ocean elected to demonstrate its power.

On February 13, the wind rose all day, the seas building higher and higher. *Tzu Hang* ran before it under her self-steering twin jibs. By 5.00 the next morning the motion was violent, the sails were thundering, and all hands went on deck to take them down. The ketch ran on under bare poles, her masts and rigging alone providing enough resistance to the wind to make her sail. Miles, at the helm, looked around at a white ocean shredded and broken by the power of the wind. A sea burst over the stern and knocked him out of the cockpit, slewing the ship sideways. Miles was still connected by his lifeline, and he scrambled up in time to straighten her up to present only her stern, the smallest possible target, to the next roaring sea. Shafts of sun broke through, and he called Guzzwell to take some movies of the most spectacular seascape he had ever seen.

Beryl relieved Miles at 9.00, bulky in oilskins, gloves and socks. Miles took a few snapshots himself, checked that she was all right, and went below. He settled himself to read in his bunk, and Pwe sat down on his stomach.

Suddenly the boat stood on its nose with a force that drove Miles' head against the bulkhead. "There was a roar of water, and I was struggling to get out of the water. It was like a submarine that had been depth-charged: completely dark, and the pressure was tremendous. Then suddenly daylight came, and I found myself up to my chest in water, with floorboards and books washing all over the place." As if from a distance he heard an anguished voice crying "Oh God, where's Bea? Where's Bea?" It was his own voice.

Tzu Hang had slewed slightly on a wave, and Beryl had corrected it, looking astern to make sure she would meet the next one exactly at right angles. What she saw was a vertical wall of water stretching from horizon to horizon, towering above *Tzu Hang* and breaking down its face like a waterfall. "I can't do anything," she thought, "I'm absolutely straight." Then she was falling, plunging in the ocean.

Tzu Hang had "pitchpoled." That extraordinary sea–and ocean sailors are still debating its origins–had lifted her stern till she ploughed her bows under and tripped on them, tumbling forwards head over heels, then falling sideways as the seven tons of lead on her keel strove to right her.

When Beryl broke water she could see no sign of the ship, and she was furious. They've left me! she thought indignantly. Then a wave lifted Beryl, and she turned, and there was *Tzu Hang*, with the wreckage of her masts tangled over the side, a six-foot square hole in the deck where her doghouse once stood, low and sluggish like a log in the water.

And John Guzzwell, having surfaced from the water in the galley, looked at her bloodstained face, her bright yellow oilskins, the white sea and the hard blue sky and thought, crazily, *what a shot for colour film!*

"This is it, you know, Miles," said Guzzwell.

"It looks like it," Miles answered.

But Beryl swam to the ship, and they held her while a wave boarded them, and hauled her aboard. "You're kneeling on my arm, John," she said. But he wasn't: she had broken her shoulder and a toe as well as suffering a deep scalp cut. "I know where the buckets are!" she announced, and suddenly the two men thought *Yes, there's a chance yet.* It had never occurred to her that there wasn't. Broken shoulder or no, Beryl baled all day, handing buckets of water to Miles on deck, while John covered the holes in the deck with locker doors and sails.

"Where's Pwe?" Miles asked.

"I can hear her from time to time," Bea answered. "She's alive. We can't do anything about her now."

They found her that evening, wet and bedraggled and cold, and all that night all four slept together for warmth. For Pwe's sake, they started the wood stove the next day, and a couple of days later they had the mess straightened out somewhat, and Guzzwell, that excellent carpenter, took the butt of the mainmast and ripped it into boards to build a makeshift mast.

"What was fantastic," Miles exclaims, "is that he still maintained his perfectionism!" And the room echoes to Bea's deep, pulsing laugh.

"He sat there," she explains, "in this *appalling* motion, sharpening his saw."

A week after the disaster, they were able to hoist some sail. The rudder was gone, and they put together a cumbersome but effective steering oar. The full story of their recovery is told in Miles' gripping book, *Once is Enough*; five weeks after the smash they sailed into Coronel, Chile, without assistance.

But once was *not* enough. For eight months, with the help of the Chilean Navy, they worked to restore *Tzu Hang*. After four months, family commitments and his own voyage took Guzzwell away, a sad parting after such closeness. The Smeetons soldiered on, and gradually admitted to one another that though they had "decided" on the safe route home, through the Panama Canal, each was still dreaming of the Horn. On December 9, 1957, they left Chile, bound south again. This time Bea and Miles were the sole crew.

"*That's* what fascinates me," I said. "After all that, how did you find it in yourselves to tackle it again?"

"Well, I don't know," shrugged Bea. "I suppose it was the way we were brought up: if you fall off a horse, you've got to get back on again. If you *don't* get back on, everyone knows you never will."

"You can't *give up*," declares Miles, as though that were the end of the matter.

How did they feel?

"Oh, not too hot!" admits Bea. "And when the gale came, we felt absolutely ghastly!"

"We never mentioned it to each other," Miles explains, "but we both felt. . .not too hot."

By Christmas day a ferocious gale had again forced them to take down all sail, and the ship lay sideways to the seas, yielding and sliding away before their force. "Lying ahull," as this is known, is a time-honoured strategy, but the Smeetons now distrust it. At 4.00 in the afternoon on Boxing Day a breaking sea took the ship in its grasp and rolled her completely over sideways.

Not again! thought Miles, *Not again!* He felt the lead keel swing above him, felt her struggle against the resistance of the spars in the water, heard the new masts snap. *Tzu Hang* found her feet, and they scrambled aft in water to their knees. Once again the doghouse was smashed in, though it was still there this time; once again the broken rigging lay in the water alongside. Once again they jury-rigged her, and once again they made a Chilean harbour without assistance, arriving in Valparaiso a month after the capsize.

"The *relief* after it happened was absolutely astounding!" Beryl laughs. "Even Pwe didn't really mind it."

Miles agrees. "It had been hanging over our heads the whole time, and it really was a tremendous relief when it happened."

Twice, it seemed, really *was* enough. *Tzu Hang* was shipped back to England on the deck of a freighter and rebuilt there. But the story goes on, chronicled by Miles in eight books. They cruised in Europe, circling the British Isles, wintering in Paris and Ibiza, then carried on right around the world through Suez and east Africa and on through the islands of southern Asia to Japan for another winter. They returned to Vancouver *via* the Aleutians, then hopped along the coast to Panama and back up the east coast to Cape Breton and the Strait of Belle Isle before making their second Atlantic crossing north of Iceland. By 1968 they were back in England.

The world of ocean cruising is a small one still, though it expands dramatically every year, and by now the Smeetons were among its most celebrated citizens, encountering friends in almost any port, climbing mountains when they could, trying languages, rounding up wandering pets, experiencing the whole globe with gusto.

"Once you've left home," says Bea, "then you might as well go on. No point in going back. Once you've sailed away from Vancouver, and even made San Francisco, why should you go back? You might just as well go on."

"Our home was aboard," Miles explains. "Everything we

were occupied with was there. And we were continually seeing new country, new people, new experiences—"

"Well, I think you've got to like travelling," Bea breaks in. "Otherwise it's no good at all—"

"We crammed so much into those years that one year seemed to be two years," Miles explains, "because there are so many new things. Here in Cochrane, time passes like a flash, because we're here the whole time. But God, when we were sailing like that, life was simply extended, wasn't it?"

"Mmm," nods Bea. "Someone would say, 'Oh, you ought to see so-and-so,' and you simply went off and saw it. No reason why you shouldn't."

By 1968, they were in their sixties, and thinking about putting down roots again. One long last cruise, perhaps. And where? To the one challenge that had defeated them: the Cape Horn passage, and this time by the most difficult route of all, from east to west against the prevailing winds and currents. Their crew was Bob Nance, a young Australian, who had rounded Cape Horn with two companions in a thirty-foot sloop a few days behind Francis Chichester.

Tzu Hang left England late that summer, called at Spain, Madeira and the Cape Verde Islands, and crossed the Atlantic to Montevideo by early November. On December 16, on a gray squally day, they gazed at "a bare, treeless headland, with bare bones of granite showing near its turreted peak. If Cape Horn is to be seen only once, this is how it should be seen, with islands and dark sounds behind it, the very tip of that great continent." The passage was not only safe and comfortable, but remarkably fast, from 50° South in the Atlantic to 50° South in the Pacific in only fourteen days.

The Smeetons have "swallowed the anchor" as the saying is, covered with honours: the Challenge Cup of England's Royal Cruising Club, the Seamanship Medal of the Liga Maritime de Chile, and in 1973 the most coveted of all, the Blue Water Medal of the Cruising Club of America. Bob Nance sails on in *Tzu Hang.* Pwe never had to use her special lifejacket after all, and she lived to an extreme old age. Clio is married, living in Sidney, B.C. Miles has a knee which no longer functions properly, Bea has lost some of the strength of her hands and this, one might think, is time for valedictory remarks.

But Bea is off to Qatar, and Miles recently took an Arctic tour on the Coast Guard icebreaker *d'Iberville*, and out in the foothills there's a game farm. "We'd like to do something for endangered species," Miles explains, taking us down to see the trumpeter swan, "but thus far we've been more involved with animals which were *individually* endangered." Two orphan moose have grown up and mated, there's a stray elk, and a few northern kit fox, an animal now extinct in Canada's wilderness. "The farm is really a hobby; we only turned over $6,000 last year. But we think of it as a kind of repayment for the pleasure we've had from animals over the years."

Beryl flings herself at a firepole and slides downstairs to feed the moose. "That unquenchable spirit of Beryl Smeeton comes from we know not where and goes we know not whither," wrote Sir Francis Chichester. "It is granted to only a few in any century. One is filled with wonder and admiration and a kind of exaltation that such women should exist in our time."

Florid, but true—and Beryl is something of a heroine to several of the most committed feminists I know. She is pleased to hear it, but she thinks the feminists "are concentrating on the wrong things. My husband washes up—who on earth cares? The thing is for him to take you seriously as an individual person, with your own interests and your own development."

Again the echo of those distant days in British India: for Bea must have sensed that in Miles she had found such a man. In the end this is a love story: an account of how two people have loved their world and the experiences it offered, how they have loved the sea and the mountains, the cat, the boat, and each other.

(April, 1976)

The Noblest Work of God:

Nobody will ever raise a vast monument to Alvin Fisher. He was not, as these things are reckoned, a great man. He commanded no armies, he held no public office, he won no honorary degrees, he built no vast fortune on the labour of other men. But the church was filled for his funeral, and his life was one of which a man could be proud.

Alvin Fisher farmed, drove a school bus, delivered mail, operated a dump truck, worked on the maintenance crew of the municipal school board of Delta, B.C., and died. A century from now he will be a yellowing photograph in a family album, a mysterious, mythical ancestor as remote from his descendants as those European immigrants who squint into the primitive cam-

A PORTRAIT OF

ALVIN FISHER

171

eras in our own family albums, posed against sod huts on the Prairies, lumber camps on the Tahsis or the Miramichi, or who sit sternly on ornate Victorian chairs, uneasy in their absurd frock-coats and ruffles.

And a small boy in California or the Yukon, who resembles Alvin in ways he will never understand, may say, "Mom, can we go to Ladner some time? I'd like to see the place our family came from."

He will never find it: Alvin's Ladner is gone already, for all practical purposes, buried by an avalanche of housing spilled over from Vancouver, sliced through by superhighways and rail lines, pock-marked by small industries, its rich black soil excavated for basements, its country roads stripped of their real names and numbered in a technocrat's fantasy of a grid which covers the whole green Fraser Valley.

Twenty years ago, one of those roads was known as the Fisher Road, and Alex Fisher, Alvin's father, was still living there on the family farm. That black soil had drawn the Fishers and the Creelmans, a generation earlier, from the tidy little farms of the Stewiacke Valley 4,000 miles east, in central Nova Scotia. On July 22, 1934, dark-haired, droll Alvin Fisher married the lithe and laughing young schoolteacher Beth Creelman. They moved in with his parents at the farm on the Fisher Road, and began a family of five children.

In 1955, when I was seventeen, a troubled city kid who had come to finish high school in a setting which might encourage me to be less of a thug than I was becoming, a happy fellow with dark curly hair and horn-rimmed glasses introduced himself to me within my first half-hour at Delta High School.

"You're new, eh?" he said. "You should meet some of the boys. I'm Keith Fisher. This is Jimmy Shields. Hey Dunbar! This character is Ray Dunbar. Bobo! Come here, will you? Bob Harding, Don Cameron. Listen, Don, what are you doing Friday night?"

"Nothin' special."

"Why don't you come to my place for supper, and we'll go to the dance in East Delta?"

Mindboggling! Nobody acted like that in Vancouver.

Thus began six months that turned my life around, six months that live in memory like a sunny island in the black sea of adolescence, six months for which I am perpetually grateful to the easygoing people of that warm Delta yesterday. Keith—or "Fish," as he was generally known—turned out to be the key to a whole community of boisterous, generous young people, and he remains one of the finest friends I have ever had. And though many of those Delta friendships have been suspended by time and distance, the tie with the Fishers has flourished.

In those days the Fishers were poor and busy. Alvin drove the school bus morning and afternoon, and while school was in session he delivered mail along one of the rural routes strung out along the back roads of that lush, flat countryside. Beth sorted mail in the post office and presided over the ramshackle, disorderly old house on Maple Road. Their eldest son, Bill, had already joined the navy and moved all the way back to Nova Scotia, where he still lives. The other four were still at home, and the family circle was generally enlarged by one or two or three stray kids, friends of one Fisher or another.

Alvin and Beth were always working, always behind. There was no time to paint the house, put away the ironing, prop up the garage. There was no money for such luxuries as a furnace: the house was heated by oil stoves and a fireplace, and in winter the upstairs bedrooms could be bitterly cold. Years later, I realized there was really no money to feed all the people like me who would drop in unannounced for a meal or a week-end; as Beth explained years later, with a rippling laugh, it meant putting a few more potatoes on and spreading the stew a bit thinner, and opening another jar of her bread-and-butter pickles, which are, I swear, the best in the world.

But there was always time for *people*: time for a visit over the crib board or for a long talk with a bewildered kid, time to pick up an elderly neighbour and drive her to a church do, time to go up to Cloverdale to visit Beth's father, time for Beth to spend at Eastern Star meetings, time for Alvin to serve the church.

The Fishers found time to have fun, time to be human. The cow was milked, the needs of the garden were met, and if the ironing wasn't put away, so what? For me, their life was a revelation. Virtue, I had concluded, was almost purely negative: don't smoke, don't drink, don't mess with girls, don't lie, don't steal, don't drive with *élan*. Perfect goodness, I suspected, was exactly the same in practice as perfect immobility or perfect boredom. I preferred to be a rascal.

Yet here were the Fishers, at once good, and interesting, and happy.

I found myself attending Ladner United Church and even, after a while, teaching Sunday School.

Sundays, indeed, were a special pleasure. Up, still groggy from a dry but lively party, briskly moving through breakfast, the house full of people looking for good shoes, a suit jacket, a matching purse. Brushes everywhere: on clothes, on hair, on shoes, on fingernails. Into Alvin's Dodge, and down the road a mile or so to the old wooden church, its interior bright with varnish, the sun streaming in through the tall eastern windows. The quiet good sense of Reverend Norman Crees' faintly English voice. My friend and mentor Nelson Allen, principal of the high school, in whose home I was living, at the organ. And the voices filling the vaulted ceiling with song:

Holy, holy, holy! Lord God Almighty,
Early in the morning our song shall rise to Theeeee....

And then back for a lunch Beth miraculously produced hot from the stove, the teasing and squabbling and the stories. *Pass us some spuds there, Miz Fudds....So he didn't know there was a T in the road, and he didn't turn left or right, he just drove straight into the ditch...Oh, I imagine you could get work with the pea-viners this summer, you should talk to Barry Etter....*And Alvin, with his white shirt and suspenders, talking quietly about why he always bought Chrysler products, and raising his voice occasionally to straighten out the behaviour of his two youngest sons.

Alvin was born a farmer, and he stayed on the family farm until 1945, when he got his own farm, which he operated for seven years. "I think it was his back gave out," remembers his son Bill. "I think he was overworked as a kid, and he never really had robust health." One way of looking at a working man's life is to say that he trades his body for his livelihood, a swap which becomes absolutely explicit in the case of Workmen's Compensation, which gives you, say, $12,000 for three fingers. Alvin was no exception. In 1952 he moved his family to the somnolent market town of Ladner, and he took up the school bus and mail route combination.

That lasted a good many years, but eventually the doctor told him to quit that, too. The hours were long, the responsibility was awesome, and anyone who has spent any amount of time driving with children must view with admiration a man who can cope with driving thirty or forty squalling, fighting, screaming practical jokers of tender years. "Yes, but Dad enjoyed that," Bill objects. Nevertheless, his nerves gave out. You could see it in him: he became more quiet than ever, but with an edge of irritability, a constantly worried face.

He bought a truck: an International tandem dump. As I heard the story from Keith, Alvin's experience at the bank tells you a good deal about his reputation.

"Hi, Alvin," said the manager, "What can we do for you today?"

"Lend me some money," Alvin smiled.

"Sure thing. How much?"

"Fifteen thousand dollars."

"It's in your account." Alvin blinked: this was 1956, when a dollar was worth something, and Alvin's house, which was his main asset, might have fetched half that much on the market.

They talked for a while. After some time, the manager said, casually, "Well, we'll fix that loan up for you. What do you want the money for, by the way?"

"A dump truck."

"Ah," said the manager. "Good for you."

The next few years were perhaps the happiest in Alvin's life. He loved his truck, which worked steadily on the highways all over southwestern B.C. Other workers on the road crew used to rag him about the care with which he treated it, the daily lube jobs, the regular washes and oil changes, the touch-up paint, the new air cleaners. "He don't need a woman," they'd say. "He's married to that truck."

He did need a woman, of course: he needed Beth, and the

175

weeks away from home were a trial. But he was making good, steady money, the children were growing up and earning their own ways, and for the first time in his life, perhaps, Alvin Fisher had a little more money than he actually required. The bank loan was shrinking. He could hire people like Keith's buddy Jimmy Shields to work a second shift with him. The Deas Island tunnel went through, and Alvin's field suddenly became valuable as a possible subdivision site. Luxuries like a holiday fell within his reach.

It seemed to me that Alvin blossomed then, developed a rich self-confidence, a sense of his own competence. He loved the wild and ragged interior of his native province, and he marvelled at the way men and machinery were transforming it, domesticating it, making it accessible. He felt himself to be at once creative and careful, a capable man working with other men on projects that would benefit the whole community.

The point is important, because this country has always—in my lifetime, at least—taken a criminal and obscene attitude toward work. Unemployment is merely a factor in a macro-economic calculus. The *quality* of work is not even a subject of discussion. "Character is formed primarily by a man's work," says E.F. Schumacher, the only writer I know who talks sense about the matter. "And work, properly conducted in conditions of human dignity and freedom, blesses those who do it and equally their products."

Alvin Fisher understood this in his bones, and when he had to sell his truck during the recession of 1960 and take a job with the School Board's maintenance crew, a certain joyful thread was drawn out of the tapestry of his life. He didn't complain. He did his work well, and he was glad to have a steady job. It was even an interesting job, much of the time. But the zest of his independence was gone, and the difference is like the difference between pleasure and the absence of pain.

It may seem that Alvin and Beth embodied a rather Presbyterian set of values, which is true—and why not? They were, after all, of solidly Presbyterian heritage, and the positive side of that plain-spoken version of Christianity offers as admirable a guide as most. Yet they avoided its characteristic excesses: they were not quick to condemn, they were not spiritually proud, they did not turn the insights of their religion into stifling rules. They always knew how to love.

The results showed up as their children matured. Most white people are, I suspect, at least tinged with racism; most Protestants probably retain a faint suspicion of Popery; most Canadians occasionally use the term "Yank" with distaste. Alvin and Beth were like the rest of us, but they were unusually hospitable to better ideas. When Keith moved to California, married a Catholic, and presented them with a cloud of American Catholic grandchildren, they were startled. When Jane married a teacher *cum* businessman of East Indian ancestry, they discovered that this had not been what they expected. When Bill marched into his forties still a bachelor, they felt, somehow, that somewhere in the world was a woman who had been deprived of a loving husband. Donald and Ken, by contrast, were relatively orthodox: Donald's wife is from Washington state but they live in Kamloops, and Ken, although he was always what Beth calls "a rebel against the old teachings," finally married a Delta girl.

The children's occupations are equally diverse. Bill is in the Coast Guard in Nova Scotia, which means I see him more often than any of the others. Keith works for a cement company in Oakland. Jane is a teacher, Donald works for a finance company, and Ken is a parts man for a diesel outfit in northern B.C.

Alvin and Beth welcomed all these diverse occupations and in-laws, and in return they have had the friendship of their children and their children's families in remarkably full measure. To my mind, their children represent their success, for the children were able to grow, to explore, to find their happiness in ways their parents could hardly have imagined, to reach across the boundaries of race, religion and nationality to form new families which have something positive to say about the unity of mankind. It is easy for clergymen and politicians to call on us to love our neighbours; it is a good deal more difficult—and a good deal more important—to raise children who will actually do it.

I remember crouching over a school atlas in the old house on Maple Road, twenty years ago, while Alvin and Beth pointed out the Nova Scotia villages their people had come from and to which

177

Bill had returned: not Stewiacke itself, but Upper Stewiacke in Beth's case, and Middle Stewiacke in Alvin's. They remembered Nova Scotia in great detail, though neither of them had seen it since early childhood: they had pictures and letters, they had family stories, and as they spoke it seemed to me that Nova Scotia must be a good deal like an older, more settled Ladner. Conversations like that, I suspect, had a good deal to do with the way I sought out the seaside province I had never seen when the time came to find my own home.

We pored over that map, with its place names as exotic as those of Europe or the South Seas, as distant and foreign as the original Scotland from which all our ancestors had come, and yet part of our own vast country: Middle Musquodoboit, Jeddore Oyster Ponds, Tangier, Mushaboom, Tatamagouche. Look at all these places, I said, all named Margaree: Margaree Forks, Upper Margaree, Big Intervale Margaree, East Margaree, North East Margaree, Margaree Harbour...

And Alvin, I remember, sighed, and confided that one of his dreams was to return to Middle Stewiacke, to visit his relatives and see where his people came from. As the years went by, the Fishers prospered. They sold the old house and built a sparkling new one in South Delta, not far from the American border. I visited them there, and saw with amusement that Beth was able, now that the children were on their own, to be the spotless housekeeper she had always wanted to be, in a house full of carpets and conveniences.

They came to Nova Scotia not once, but four or five times—and the ironies turned again. For Ladner, now that prosperity had struck it, was no longer the farming and fishing village that once dreamed beside the muddy back channels of the Fraser. Ladner had become a bedroom suburb, with shopping malls and manicured lawns, where the lowing of cattle had given way to the *staccato* bark of the power mower. But Middle Stewiacke had not changed; not in ten years, not in fifty, so far as its basic lifestyle was concerned. Middle Stewiacke was more like Ladner than Ladner itself. Alvin and Beth bought a lot, and planned to retire there.

Instead, Alvin suffered perhaps the most cruel cut of all. In

February, 1973, he was working on a scaffolding tucked under the ceiling of the gymnasium at North Delta High School, when one of his fellow workers heard a soft, heavy thud. He turned, and there, forty feet below, lay Alvin, crumpled on the floor. He was rushed to hospital, in critical condition. He had a fractured skull and brain injuries, and he lay in a coma for several weeks, his life very much in question, while his children gathered from across the continent.

What had happened? Nobody will ever really know, but the doctors guessed that for some reason he had simply blacked out. He fell without a cry, and he never recovered his memory enough to say what he had experienced. Though he did recover remarkably, he was never quite the same. He was short-tempered, he suffered from blinding headaches, and his memory was spotty, though it returned more and more fully as the months went by.

For Beth, it was a strange and difficult time. Nobody ever knows what someone else's marriage is like, but so far as I could judge the two of them had been deeply in love for forty years, aiding and comforting one another through a life that was never easy. One of the most poignant images I know is that of Alvin, bandaged and dazed, wandering out of the hospital and into the streets of New Westminster, longingly searching for Beth.

When I met them, they were in their early forties, and the roundedness of their feeling for one another shaped the whole happy atmosphere of their home. I remember Beth once telling me they knew one another so well, and were so thoroughly content with one another's company, that their communion often went on most powerfully without the use even of words. "We can drive along for miles and miles in the car," she said happily, "without saying anything, just enjoying the pleasure of being together."

The accident shattered that graceful, easy communion, and Beth became something more like a mother to a rather irascible boy. It must have been a disorienting and painful experience, living with a man who was not quite Alvin, a man distinctly less considerate and perceptive than the man with whom she had built her life. Yet they fought it through together, and every time

179

I saw them—once or twice a year—Alvin had made some more progress, had passed through another stage of his recovery, was taking occupational therapy, had been able to go back to work.

He worked until January, 1977, though he was increasingly troubled by pains in his shoulder and upper back. He went back into hospital, and was found to have cancer both in his prostate gland and in his bones. The treatment appeared to be damaging his liver—but later the doctors discovered his liver had also been full of cancer.

For three weeks Beth went to the hospital every day, often accompanied by her sister Alice and her closest friend, Sydna Mole. She sat with Alvin, talked with him when he was conscious, did her knitting or silently held his hand when he was not. And then, one day, "he gave a little twist of his face, and he was gone."

Jane played the organ at his funeral, and his family filled a third of the church. It was not a mourning of his death, my mother reported, but a celebration of his life, "a happy service, which was what the Fishers had wanted." Al Skinner, the young Nova Scotian minister who had replaced Norman Crees, described this life, so rich in affection, endurance and accomplishment, and remarked in passing that Alvin had worked the week before he went into the hospital. And the music was in keeping:

Dance, dance, wherever you may be!
I am the Lord of the Dance, said He,
And I lead you all, wherever you may be,
And I lead you all in the dance, said He!

The King of Saudi Arabia died a little before Alvin, and the German-American rocket expert Werner Von Braun a little after. They had made their marks on history, and their deaths were widely noted. Alvin's was not, but his is the greater legacy. For he, and not they, offers some reason to hope that humanity may, despite its follies, at length acquit itself with honour in the judgment of the universe.

(July, 1977)

The Children
of Terror

In memory I see them clearly even over twenty intervening years: some of the men in beards, most in overalls, their wives in heavy coats and Russian headscarves, standing beside their old cars and pickup trucks in the roadside fir trees. The sanatorium was down on the lakeshore, and the road passed it perhaps twenty feet up the mountainside.

The Doukhobor parents gathered at the head of the driveway and began moving down towards the sanatorium, walking close together. Suddenly a great sacred chord burst from them, as though driven from a pipe organ, and they settled into a majestic hymn, solid as the cordilleran mountains behind them, tempestuous as the ruffled surface of the grey autumn lake they faced.

Powerful, dignified and serene, the music enfolded the waiting children, reverberated through the sanatorium, lost itself in the vast mountain landscape.

At the wire fence their song ended, their formation dissolved, and they rushed to greet their imprisoned children. They wept, chattered, cried endearments in Russian. They passed gifts and treats over the fence, tried to kiss through the wire, prayed by the little table with the bread, salt and water, the Doukhobor symbols of life.

They were Sons of Freedom, the small radical group of Doukhobors who had already become notorious for bombing, burning and nude parades of protest, much to the embarrassment of the vast majority of Doukhobors who called themselves Orthodox or Independent. The Sons of Freedom had resolutely refused to send their children to school, and the new Social Credit government of British Columbia had responded, in September, 1953, by seizing 104 truant children, making them wards of the province, and installing them in the disused TB sanatorium at New Denver, deep in the mountains of the West Kootenays, sixty or eighty or a hundred miles from the Freedomite centres of Krestova, Thrums, Shoreacres, Gilpin, Grand Forks.

During school hours, the children attended the New Denver public schools; the rest of their time was spent in the New Denver School Dormitory, as the san was renamed, in activities organized by the dormitory staff. They would remain in the dorm till they turned fifteen. On the first and third Sunday of each month, their parents were allowed to pay them a visit.

"It's a harsh course, but what's the alternative?" asked Attorney-General Robert Bonner. "No exceptions can be made. I myself would be in trouble if I didn't send my children to school."

What effect would the dorm have? Freedomite spokesmen claimed it was breeding a whole new generation of resentful terrorists: the government was, after all, clearly demonstrating its oppressiveness during the children's most formative years. School Superintendent Nelson Allen, like most officials, disagreed. "When the children leave after eight years," he told a reporter, "they'll no longer be Sons of Freedom. They'll be Canadians."

Nelson Allen is no authoritarian monster: he is one of the finest men I have ever known, and I have known him since I was two years old. I lived for six months in his home, and graduated from a high school of which he was the principal. Two years later he hired me to teach junior high in New Denver. Eight of my students were Freedomite children.

What *did* happen to them?

Over the years I have wondered about it often, as attitudes the Doukhobors have always held gradually began replacing the received opinions of the 'fifties. Non-Doukhobors have been going back to the land, committed to manual labour and simple communal living. Vietnam produced a great revulsion against war. Many of us, like the Doukhobors, don't register our marriages any more. We agree that too many possessions are impediments, concealing from us the real quality of human life. My own children don't attend the public schools. A good many non-Doukhobors have given up smoking and eating meat.

In 1957, I was not particularly critical of the Dormitory. I was ignorant and ambitious, frightened by my responsibilities, more than a trifle authoritarian myself. But, like many Canadians, I have since moved towards the Doukhobors in my outlook. Have they moved towards us?

And what has happened to the Sons of Freedom in particular? Enigmatic and unpredictable, radically democratic in principle but in practice always given to following strong leaders, have the Sons of Freedom found some equilibrium?

I knew that three of the most contentious issues had been settled. Doukhobors have always maintained that they could give allegiance only to the spirit of Christ which is within every man and woman, and that other authority was irrelevant at best, evil at worst. Hence, Orthodox and Freedomites alike refused to take oaths of allegiance, to become citizens, to register births, deaths and marriages. Through a simple rephrasing worked out by Magistrate William Evans of Nelson, that series of problems seems to have been solved.

"I went to Veregin"–John J. Veregin, leader of the Orthodox Doukhobors–"and said, Look here, what exactly is the problem?" recalls Evans, now enjoying retirement on Vancouver Island. "'Well,' he said, 'where it says *citizenship* you've got *Ca-*

nadian. But we're not Canadian, we're citizens of Christ.' Well, I said, what about *Canadian, subject to the laws of Jesus Christ* or something like that? Oh, well, that'd be all right. Such a simple thing, really. But it made all the difference. After that we back-registered the marriages of 2,000 couples or so.

"Then the land question." The Doukhobor lands in interior B.C. had been taken over by the province in the 'thirties, after the bankruptcy of the Christian Community of Universal Brotherhood, the Doukhobor commune of several thousand people which owned farms, sawmills, brickyards and other enterprises worth perhaps $3 million. The government intervened to save the Doukhobors from eviction, but did nothing to salvage the Community itself, and many Doukhobors saw the events as a plot to steal their land. They refused to buy it back as individuals, and the matter remained to vex everyone for over twenty years.

In 1961, Magistrate Evans was asked to try to settle it. He won the support of Veregin, and that of Stefan Sorokin, spiritual leader of the Sons of Freedom, who wrote from his home in Uruguay to instruct his followers not to interfere with the sale. In the complex world of Doukhobor affairs, Sorokin is a shadowy, mysterious figure. For years he was reviled by outsiders as a char-latan, an imposter and a racketeer; more recently he has won considerable respect–from Evans, among others–for his part in bringing the Freedomites to terms with the context in which they live.

As the sales progressed, some acts of terrorism did take place, the worst being the burning of the whole village of Ooteshenie that August. But ultimately the Sons of Freedom even bought the land in Krestova themselves, and began for the first time to erect permanent homes rather than the tarpaper shacks which once characterized the village.

And the Dormitory was closed in 1959, when the mothers of the children appeared before Evans to give their promise that their children would attend school that fall. Not everyone was–or is–happy about it, but the Freedomites apparently concluded that they really had no choice.

In 1962, roughly 200 Freedomite men were being held in a

specially-created prison at Agassiz, 90 miles up the Fraser River from Vancouver. That summer, under the leadership of a formidable woman named Florence Storgeoff (or "Big Fanny," as she came to be known), 600 Sons of Freedom trekked out of Krestova to set up a vigil before the prison. It took them nearly a year to get there, after being twice halted by the police and wintering in Vancouver. But they were profoundly affected by the city and by non-Doukhobors whose patience had not been worn thin by two generations of conflict in the Kootenays. The trek to Agassiz may have been the last great act of Freedomite rebellion. Some of its participants are still at the coast and in the Fraser Valley; most have trickled home.

"I'd like to look up my eight kids and see what's happened to them," I told Nelson and Elaine Allen, as we dined in the home to which they have retired, high on the slopes of West Vancouver. "You know, I've become pretty sympathetic to a lot of Doukhobor ideas."

"I think we all have," said Nelson Allen.

They weren't hard to find. One of them is dead: Mary Kalmakoff, killed in 1965 when the side of a mountain slid across the Hope-Princeton Highway, burying the car in which she was travelling. One is in Vancouver, one in northern B.C., one in Grand Forks, and the other four are all in or near Krestova.

I sat with Terry Reibin in a tavern in a raw northern town. (I've changed all the names except Mary's.) I remembered him as a happy-go-lucky boy, quick-witted and friendly, with a passion for Johnny Cash. He grinned, and admitted he was a good enough musician to get paid for it; his guitar still gets him a standing invitation to all the best parties.

New Denver is "away in the past, I don't think about it very often. I look towards the future. But it was hell, for me. Really, every day was hell. I tried to run away once, with three or four other guys, but we got as far as the lookout just out of town and it started to rain and we gave up. If you're stuck in there, you might as well get along with the staff; if you don't, you'll only spend your time haulin' rocks." He laughed, a brief, unamused snort.

185

Hauling rocks?

Terry shifted in his chair, swivelled to greet a couple of passing Indians. "Most of my friends up here are Indians, you know that? Well, haulin' rocks: once a couple of us got caught stealing fishing tackle out of one of the little shacks down by the shore. You remember the little rock wall around the dorm? Well, we spent the whole summer one year haulin' rocks for that in our wheelbarrow. Time off to eat, then back to work without even a rest. What a hell of a summer that was! All the other kids swimming and us haulin' rocks. It was torture."

He liked school, and was attending school anyway when the dorm was set up, at which point his parents took him *out* of school, to show their solidarity with the other Sons of Freedom. "I used to run away and try to go to school," Terry said, "and my mother would run after me and bring me back. Ah, that stupid, silly religion! After I got out I didn't want nothin' to do with it, I went to the Cariboo with my brother and went to Grade 9." He quit school and tried to join the Air Force–the *Air Force*? "I wanted to fly jets," he grinned. "All my life, ever since I was little, I wanted to fly jets." But he was too young.

He went to work as a carpenter and cabinetmaker, married a Catholic girl (over her parents' strong objections, others told me) and fathered two children. He also became a very heavy drinker, and the marriage ultimately disintegrated. "The drinking was part of the reason for the divorce," he conceded. "I thought of joining AA, but I thought No, if I can't control it by myself–and I have–I really have. I can get along just fine without booze.

"But I'm broke. I had a 12' by 62' house trailer, a pickup and a car, but now the heat is cut off, I'm behind in my rent, and I owe money to my friends. There were so many strikes around here this past year there just *wasn't* any work. Things are looking better now; if the weather holds, I'll be getting to work next week. We're building a house, and the owner ran out of money. But she's supposed to be getting some more money now. Man, it's a monstrous house..."

We crossed the street to a restaurant, grabbed a snack before I boarded my bus. I kept looking at this husky, handsome man, superimposed on the boy I had known. The same humour, the same quick smile, the same common sense. When he was fourteen and I was twenty, the gap between us was enormous. Now he's thirty-three and I'm thirty-nine, and we're basically the same age, with the same perplexities, the same enjoyments. I liked him then, I like him now.

It's ironic, I thought as the bus pulled away, that Terry, who seemed the most self-confident and relaxed of them all, was probably hurt the most, and has certainly had the roughest life.

Pete Stoochnoff was in the Interior when I was in Vancouver, in Vancouver when I was in the Interior. We finally settled for a phone call.

Pete's education ended when he left my Grade 7 class, and there was no work in the Kootenays for uneducated men. He migrated back and forth to more prosperous parts of the province, and in 1962 found a home for two full years in prison, convicted of conspiracy to commit arson. After that he went to Vancouver, where his uncle got him into a construction union.

"Since then I've made good steady progress," he said proudly. "I've been eight years with this one company, and now I'm supervising their whole job up here in the Cariboo. I've been married for eight years, too. We've got two kids, five and three, and a nice house in the suburbs. I wish you could see it. My wife was raised Anglican.

"I'm still a Doukhobor, sure. I don't practise it, but I don't hide it. I try to keep to the ideals as much as I can. I can live like this and still believe this way—you know, I don't have to go and take my clothes off."

He does eat meat now, though—"I didn't like it at first"—but they also put in a garden. "It's a big thing with us, the garden." And the old Doukhobor slogan "hard work and peaceful life" still sums up the way he wants to live.

What about New Denver? "I don't hold grudges. Time mellows it. You feel kind of unfortunate that it did happen, but I probably wouldn't have gone to school otherwise, and the educational value was great. But it was hard on the parents, and hard on the kids. Any time you had a problem you felt pretty rough, you know, you can't ask a matron; *they* don't care.

187

"I think the government intended to break up the religion a bit, and I think they succeeded. But some of the kids hardened, mind you."

Indeed they did. Several of the kids from New Denver, like Pete, served jail time after their release; one at least, Harry Kootnikoff, blew himself up with his home-made bomb at the age of seventeen.

Pete, I said, how would you sum up your life now? Are you happy? And the answer came back over the telephone as quick as a smile.

"Yes, since I've been married."

I found Bill Berisoff by looking him up in the Grand Forks' phone book. I called him from Ike's Cafe, where they serve vegetable plates, meatless hamburgers, and excellent borsch. "Bless our food and the guests we serve," says the menu. Bill came round and took me to his house, a pleasant, simple bungalow he built himself, with the help of his father and brother. He's worked in a local wood-processing plant virtually since he left New Denver. He's a bit heavier, he's lost a finger and grown a nice moustache, but otherwise he's changed surprisingly little since then.

His wife, Anna, was an Orthodox Doukhobor, "but we're really nowhere now," said Bill, pouring us all Screwdrivers. "We're neither one or the other, and I think my parents are pretty much the same. We're Doukhobors, all right, we believe in the Doukhobor way of life—"

"What's the Orthodox slogan?" said Anna. "Toil and peaceful life. That's all."

They have a large garden, they do a lot of canning, and they would like to move out into the country, get a cow and a few chickens and grow a bit more food than they do: the old Doukhobor affection for the land remains. But they aren't at all interested in communal living. It has its attractions, Anna admits, but "I've really come to like my privacy."

"I'm glad I went to school," said Bill, in his quiet, thoughtful way. "I only wish I'd gone further. I went down to Vancouver Vocational Institute a few years ago for four months, and in that four months I took four grades of school, and got my Grade 10. They were amazed at that, but I really wanted to learn. It wasn't for an apprenticeship or anything, I just wanted to have my Grade 10. In the old days, on the community farms, you didn't need an education, but if you're going to get a job today, you've got to have some."

So New Denver didn't make him more radical?

"Maybe after you came out of the school you were a bit more wild and extreme for two or three years, but after a while you've got to grow up and calm down," he grinned. "We have to send our kids to school, we've learned that. And the land isn't a big thing any more, it's all been subdivided and sold. That makes it hard to have a communal life even if you wanted to, and it's one of the big things that was always a cause of trouble."

I had been thinking about the causes of trouble, and it seemed to me that the only one which would really set the Kootenays afire again would be conscription into the armed forces.

"Yes!" said Bill, with energy, "and then it wouldn't be just the Sons of Freedom, it would be the Orthodox and a lot of people who aren't Doukhobors at all, too."

"The old basic Doukhobor religion is really gone," said Anna. "You know, most Doukhobors live like most other Canadians."

"I think we'll join the hippies," Bill grinned. "They're doing what the Sons of Freedom always wanted to do. But I think the Sons of Freedom were better dressed."

"And cleaner," sniffed Anna, primly. And we all laughed.

I found Valerie Sherstobitoff in a little wooden house at Shore-acres, a big cheerful woman of thirty-two with only one of her three kids still under school age. She spent five years in the dorm—like Terry, she was going to school before the trouble started, and was pulled out by her parents. When she got out, she married her next-door neighbour Alex at seventeen, had her first child at eighteen. Alex spent five years in the prison at Agassiz, and Valerie stood the long vigil outside the prison. Then they worked in Vancouver for five years, "until we got tired of the rat race."

"After five years in the san, and five years in Agassiz for Alex, we're just tired. The Sons of Freedom are up the hill there in Krestova, and the people down here are pretty well all Orthodox, and we're neither. I tell Alex, if we live a Christian life in our own home, take care of our kids and love one another, what God is going to do anything to us, eh?''

She laughed, poured a cup of coffee, sat down at the kitchen table. Vanya, her four-year-old son, was engrossed in TV in the living room.

"In the dorm we used to gather together every night in a half-circle around the bread, salt and water, and pray. Sometimes we'd strip and pray. Then before bed every night we'd pray and pray beside the beds. Imagine, little kids of ten and eleven, where did we get all that? Now I can't even teach those prayers to my children because I don't *know* them any more. I never pray now except when I've got trouble; and that's *bad*, just to pray when you need help.

"But I'll tell you, I don't regret any of it. I learned to read and write a little, and it's only my fault that I didn't insist on going to school after I came home."

A bright winter morning, the sun bouncing off the snow and in through the windows; and I had a curious sense of homecoming. Valerie was unreachable in school, very quiet and withdrawn, at times mildly amused, at times almost sullen. And yet somehow this outgoing, happy woman was hiding inside there too. We weren't close then, but it seems natural to feel close now. I never met Alex, who's away working as a labourer on one of the Columbia River hydro dams, but I'm sure I'd like him. How much of the old Doukhobor life do they retain?

"Well, we have a big garden, and we can everything. We start in April with hotbeds. I'd like to have a cow for the milk and butter and cheese. We do eat meat, but not too much, with all you hear about what's in it. But I make our bread and jam, and when I give the kids a jam sandwich I feel good about it, because I know everything that's in it.

"But Shoreacres has changed. It's not as friendly now, and that's because of the telephone. Before, if you wanted to talk to someone you got dressed up and went to see them. Now you call them on the phone and you never get outside all winter. And it seems like everyone's holding onto material things now, keeping up with the Joneses. I guess it's the same in every community, you have a group that's got all the electric appliances and the car and the house and if you don't have all that you're not one of them."

Vanya came in: *Sesame Street* was over, he was hungry. Valerie made him a jam sandwich, and gave me one. It really *was* good.

"Why'd you put butter on my sandwich?" Vanya asked, biting into it.

"To make you nice and chubby," grinned Valerie. "You know, there's something: I see the French being taught on TV, and I think, gee, I wish that was Russian. They do teach Russian in the schools here, but the TV comes from Vancouver and Spokane."

The children weren't registered, and Valerie wasn't getting family allowance, so the probation officer convinced her to register them. But their marriage still isn't registered. Valerie laughed heartily, but her eyes were flashing. "I told him, do I need a piece of paper to say I want to live with Alex, I want to bear his children and love him? What does the paper do? Well, he took off without another word. But in a way I can see it. I have an aunt a little older than I am, and her husband was killed and she had a difficult time to get their property."

But that only means he needed a will, not a registered marriage.

"Yes, and his brother was after him to do it six months before he died. But it worked out. Anyway she got another man."

She mentioned the principal of the high school where I taught. "I always thought he was prejudiced against the Doukhobors. And then that Army stuff, always so smart making his little salutes, and the town kids so proud of their army uniforms—ugh!"

It's true: the man *was* prejudiced against the Doukhobors: in private he would talk about them in ways that would blister paint. He was also a Captain in the Reserve Army, and he drilled a company of cadets in the school gymnasium. Why were we so willing to affront Doukhobor values? Why did we have to raise the flag and lower it every day? Why could we not have had at least one Russian-speaking teacher, and a few classes in Russian?

191

Why did we offer no courses in agriculture? These things existed in the B.C. school curriculum of the day, but not in the little high school in New Denver.

Nelson Allen was taken aback to hear about the army drills; he hadn't at the time realized what was happening. And he pointed out that he was given extra money to hire extra teachers because of the Freedomite kids, but not extra money to establish special programs for them.

"They could have left the Doukhobors alone: they would have wised up on their own after a while," Valerie muses. "Or we could have had schools of our own right in the communities. All the money they spent!

"I was in New Denver once afterwards. We were coming home from the coast, and my husband said, 'Let's go over the Monashee through Nakusp and New Denver.' I said Sure, but when we got to New Denver my heart was pounding, and I was hot and breathless, and I said, Let's go, get me out of here. I don't know why that was, but you know–five years out of your life is a long time."

You don't smoke in Marlene's spotless house, but you can have a beer if you want. Marlene and George Tarasoff aren't Doukhobors any more: they're Jehovah's Witnesses, members of the one sect to make any inroads among the "Spirit Wrestlers," which is what "Doukhobor" literally means. George built the house himself over the fifteen years of their marriage; they first set up housekeeping in the little log house that stands next door, and they're clearly proud of their progress. Deep shag carpets, old brick and green-stained cedar, a Franklin stove on a brick foundation. They have two boys, twelve and ten.

Marlene greeted me warmly but remained a bit suspicious, wanted to be sure that her welfare and her family's couldn't possibly be damaged by anything I might write. After my phone call, she had checked her old autograph book, and there, sure enough, was a bit of doggerel verse and my signature, twenty years ago. Like several of the others, she remembered me primarily as a music teacher, though in fact music was a relatively minor part of my job.

She remembered the dorm as "very strict. You learned discipline. Each day we woke up at seven, did our chores; some cleared out the cubicles, some cleaned the washrooms, some peeled potatoes. Then breakfast and off to school. We were in good shape, you know, we walked to school and back twice a day, had gym twice a week at the dorm as well as all the activities at the school.

"I liked school, but I couldn't wait to get out. Grade 7 was as far as I ever went. I didn't have the maturity to insist on going back, and you didn't get any support from anyone else." She too was going to school and was pulled out when the trouble started. One night the house was surrounded by Mounties who took her with her brother and sister to Nelson. There they were handed over to a man and woman, social workers who took them "on that long car ride to New Denver. The Mounties were very polite and these people were very kind and gentle. I remember they bought us chocolate bars.

"I don't blame my parents for it. They were doing the right thing according to their religion." Does she blame the government? "Well, the law says children have to go to school. What was the alternative?"

George is of Orthodox background, and when the 1962 trek was forming up he was in hospital with a broken leg; he asked to get out early to be sure Marlene didn't go. She didn't, though her brother and sister did.

"Even then I was questioning my religion," she told me. "We memorized the psalms, but what did it mean? I began checking it with the Bible and it didn't add up. Things were left out. Then in 1974 I became a Jehovah's Witness. Now I feel hope. I didn't feel any hope before."

She gave me a few leaflets: *Awake, The Watchtower*. I promised to read them, and I did. But they didn't speak to me as they do to her.

The Novai Pasolick, the New Settlement, is tucked away up a little valley in the hills behind Krestova, and here I found my last two students, Joe Maloff and Nick Kapustin. I actually caught Joe at the end of a hockey practice in Nelson: he's thirty-two, a big chunk of a man who also works on a dam and gets home only on the week-ends. It was a fleeting talk.

He did thirty months in Agassiz for conspiracy to commit ar-son, and he says New Denver "didn't change me. I'll always be the same. I don't regret anything. If I had to do it again I'd do everything the same."

But he didn't care for prison. "I'd see that big moon shining through the mist and I'd feel like going for a walk, but you couldn't. And you'd really notice things you always took for granted—the green of the trees—or something. But I'd do it again if I had to. It depends on what you're fighting for."

He has three kids, and they go to school. "I don't really believe in it, but what can you do? You're caught up in the cogs of a big machine. Look, I gotta go. Come around sometime; you're al-ways welcome."

You enter the Novai Pasolick by a dirt road off a dirt road, in what appears to be an uninhabited valley. The road climbs a few feet to a level shelf, and forks: and all around you, suddenly, are trim little wooden houses tucked in among the towering ever-greens, fifty or sixty of them, all built on one piece of land owned in trust by four members. There's no electricity, no telephone, no sewers; running water comes from a creek above the settle-ment and is piped into the houses and bath-houses. And one of these quite charming houses, with trees virtually sweeping its eaves, is Nick's.

He was a tiny kid, Nick, bright-eyed and bespectacled, with an impish sense of humour and an irrepressible intelligence. Now he's a very big man, 195 pounds, with powerful shoulders and no fat. He worked about four and a half months last year as a car-penter, earned "six or seven thousand," and with his lifestyle that was enough for himself, his lovely wife Lillian, and their five children. He built the house—or rather, is building it—himself. He's a good carpenter and an inspired scrounger: the beautiful V-joint ceiling, he tells me, is made of cheap cedar that he picked up for $65.00 a thousand; the root cellar is lined with cull 2″ x 8″ he bought for only $10.00 a thousand, "though lots of it really was junk; we used it for firewood."

They don't eat meat, don't smoke, don't drink, though

they've tried all three. "People talk about a good big steak," Nick puzzles, "but it does nothing for me."

"You can't chew it," Lillian shrugs. "It's like rubber." The children ate meat in Vancouver, but they don't miss it much. "They understand that to eat it you have to kill animals," Lillian explains.

They went on the great trek to Agassiz, and lived in Vancouver for ten years. They bought a house, filled it with appliances, tried to be modern and urban, and they have some amusing stories about finding their way around at first, as well as some stories they take as object lessons about city life: its violence, its impersonality, its individualism.

"That life is empty," Nick declares. "I had a pretty responsible job, but I'd go up thirty-one storeys in an elevator with the same guys every morning and we'd just nod and say, 'Rainy today,' or 'Nice morning.' So one day, four years ago, I told the company that I wasn't going to supervise any more, that I'd work another month for them just as a carpenter and that's it. At that point we came home. Will you stay for supper?"

Sure, love to. It turns out to be superb: borsch made with spinach and spiced with garlic, home-made bread, pyrohi (a pastry stuffed with cheese, peas or sauerkraut), pickles and apple pie with rye crust—Lillian's first rye crust, and a great success. Nick grins that he's twenty pounds heavier than he'd like to be. "It's her fault." She scowls at the food we haven't eaten, even though we're groaningly full. "You two didn't eat much," she observes.

Nick continues to be a great reader, though he's mildly embarrassed about it: he spends a lot of time reading that could go into productive work. It's a family joke. Ask him to do something, and he says, "I'll do it when I finish my reading." What does he read? "Some junk, occult stuff, science fiction. Herman Hesse, Scott, Tolstoy, Dostoevsky. Useful books, like *Diet for a Small Planet.*"

It's one of those occasions in which the details matter less than the mood. The evening falls, and Nick lights the propane lamps: a warm glow from the natural wood all around us. The house is completely insulated, heated by an oil space heater. The stove is propane. They don't miss the city services. But the warmth in the

195

house is not just a matter of BTUs; it has to do with a man and his wife, their kids, their community; it has to do with friendships renewed and extended.

The next day, Sunday, Nick took me to a *sobraniye* in Krestova. "Don't be surprised if a few old girls take their clothes off, because there's an outsider there," Nick smiled. "You know, you're still among the Sons of Freedom." In a plain building the people separated, the men and boys to one side, the women and girls to the other. A small table with bread, salt and water stood between them. As each person entered, he bowed low and said, "*Slava bohu*": Glory to God. The others bowed in return and replied, "*Kristos vas kres*": Christ is risen. These bows are the one truly ceremonial act in the faith: the recognition of the spark of God which is in every human being.

The service itself consisted of psalms and hymns, the psalms recited by memory, first by the men and boys, then by the women and girls. When the children would falter, several voices would unhurriedly prompt them. *Kristos vas kres* rang out like a refrain at several points: I noticed it had ended Nick's blessing at supper, too.

And the singing, that magnificent choral singing. Totally unaccompanied, sounding as though God himself were playing a single instrument made up of His people in Krestova, the singing was enough to make you shiver with its passion and steady belief; and during the singing four or five elderly women did strip in that symbolic Freedomite gesture of ridding oneself of all the tentacles of material possessions, returning to the state in which everyone entered the world. They were tucked away in a back row, and their action wasn't very conspicuous, but it did remind the outsider—as though the *sobraniye* itself wouldn't have—that these were indeed the Sons of Freedom. Women naked, and signs on the walls: NO OTHER RELIGIOUS ORGANIZATION HAS ITS OWN POLICE FORCE, WHY MUST WE? in reference to the RCMP "D" (for Doukhobor) Squad, which still exists in Nelson. SONS OF FREEDOM CANNOT BE SLAVES OF CORRUPTION. THE WELFARE OF THE WORLD IS NOT WORTH THE SACRIFICE OF A SINGLE CHILD.

The hymns and psalms are traditional, and are the only means by which the essentials of the faith are passed on from generation to generation in a peasant culture without books. Nick knows sixty or seventy, and knew twenty-seven before he went to New Denver. That's not to say traditional Doukhobors are necessarily illiterate. "You take my father-in-law, now, he'd show up statistically as illiterate. He's never had a day's schooling in his life, officially," Nick told me. "But he's perfectly literate in his own language; he reads Tolstoy and Dostoevsky and Bunyan in Russian, and he's a man of considerable depth and learning."

The service ended, we shook hands with a few people and left. "There's no pressure to attend," said Nick. "I try to go pretty regularly. But the thing is to live your religion in your daily life, and the only judges of that are you and God."

And New Denver? Last year Nick worked on the old san, which was being converted into a senior citizens' personal care centre. "That was a funny feeling," he mused. "But we changed it so there wasn't much to remember but the attic. I remember crawling around in the attic; we weren't supposed to go up there, but we did.

"I don't feel any bitterness, there's no point feeling bitter. I think I would have turned out pretty much the same whether I'd gone there or not.

"You know, there were all kinds of people manipulating the Sons of Freedom in the old days. They were simple, ignorant people; you could tell them anything and they'd believe it. And then there was this prophecy that we'd return to Mother Russia, that we'd emigrate through the jails. Well, how are you going to make this prophecy come true? You've got to get into jail. So all kinds of people pleaded guilty to things they had nothing to do with, and people would testify against them just to get them into jail. Joe Maloff spent five years in Agassiz; he burned down some old shack somewhere to do his part.

"But now, we call ourselves the Community of Reformed Doukhobors, and we've put out a statement that anyone who has anything to do with bombs, burning, guns or violence is automatically excluded from membership. We've been manipulated by the left and jailed by the right, but basically we have nothing to do with politics. We're Doukhobors, right? It's between us and

Mother Earth, and that's it."

With his dark, slim wife and a couple of the older children, we walked out into the snowy night to pick up the younger ones at Lillian's parents' house. The pine trees soared above us, their branches tufted with snow, their tips pointing to a sky scattered with stars. There wasn't a breath of wind. Our boots squeaked in the snow, and through the thick woods came the winking, the soft gas lights of the harboured houses.

"Beautiful, eh?" said Nick. "Listen. Stop, listen." We did. "You can't hear a sound." He pointed out the houses: practically every one had one parent or another at New Denver. Lillian laughed. She was never caught: when the Mounties came, she hid in a false wall that her father had built.

After all that turmoil, this peace. Krestova, it seemed to me, had a lot more to tell other Canadians than we used to think. Perhaps the Novai Pasolick represented the harmonizing of the old Doukhobor ideals with the conditions of modern Canada, the advancing edge of an old faith.

"A number of people have said that," Nick nodded thoughtfully. "In fact I think the NDP government saw us that way." He paused, looked around at the quiet mountain village, and spoke very softly.

"We'd be very proud if it were true."

(September, 1976)

Seasons
in the Rain

The first thing to understand about Vancouver is that the climate is not very pleasant.

Vancouverites loudly proclaim the precise opposite. Persons who express doubt about the climate are barred from voting in municipal elections. Visitors who wonder absently what happened to the sun are quick-frozen and shipped C.O.D. to Moose Jaw. As you approach Vancouver International Airport large signs are seen on the mountaintops. THE WEATHER HERE, they say, IS WONDERFUL.

On the subject of climate, all Vancouverites are shameless, brazen, unblinking liars.

The climate in Vancouver is terrible. The rains begin in Van-

couver at the beginning of September. They continue virtually unbroken till the end of the following August. Then nature's inexorable cycle repeats itself, and another year's growth of green moist moss begins growing on everyone's hair.

Relatively few people use umbrellas, because of the mad theory that the climate is pleasant. Instead, they develop The Vancouver Slouch. Heads and shoulders hunched forward, white wrinkled hands thrust deep into their pockets, they pad onward through the water, offering only their backs to the rain. In their hearts they know the rain will never stop. With their voices they lie. Their rounded shoulders tell the truth.

I was reared in Vancouver. I am giving it to you straight. My posture still leaves a great deal to be desired.

When I first moved east of the Rockies to live, I was twenty-seven years old. In the opinion of a true Vancouverite, the rest of Canada is barely worth selling for junk: a vast freezing wilderness of whining wheat farmers, arrogant bureaucrats, carnivorous stockbrokers and raving separatists. Naturally I skipped all that and went direct to London, England. One day my family and I emerged from King's Cross railway station, half a dozen blocks from home. It was pouring down rain: torrents, buckets, cascades of flying water. We raced down the street past the grubby brick buildings, all alone on the checkerboard sidewalks. Astonished Londoners, huddled in doorways, gaped at us as we zipped past. The baby's stroller clattered and banged, our coats flew open, we gasped for breath. As we rounded the last corner for home, the rain stopped. The sky cleared. The sun shone brilliantly. The Englishmen stepped jauntily out of their doorways and strode along their ways, swinging their furled umbrellas.

You see? You see? We were Vancouverites. The notion that the rain might *stop* was as foreign and incomprehensible as half-crowns and florins.

Aside from their outrageous falsehoods about the climate, Vancouverites are exceptionally pleasant. Born Vancouverites are not, however, easy to find.

My mother came to Vancouver from a farm in Manitoba. My father came from North Bay, Ontario, *via* the Interior of B.C. The man who for a generation spoke stridently for the province of the setting sun, W.A.C. Bennett, came from Hampton, New Brunswick. The first premier of B.C., a chap named Smith who took the wonderful name Amor de Cosmos, Lover of the Universe, was a visionary Nova Scotian.

Appropriately enough, Vancouver has one of the largest Chinatowns in the Western world, a marvellously exotic enclave around Pender and Main of which the city has at last learned to be proud. Wander into a Pender Street import store, and emerge with brass Buddhas, delicate parasols, folding fans, bamboo snakes, china soup bowls with china spoons. The whole package is unlikely to cost fifteen dollars. Then wander to Ming's or the Ho Inn, the Yen Lock or the Bamboo Terrace or any of the other restaurants nearby, and dine splendidly for three or four dollars.

Notice the pagoda-roofed telephone booth, and pay some attention to the tops of the tall, narrow buildings, with their balconies and Chinese flourishes. Leading up to them are shabby staircases, with excited Asian voices floating down to the street. Passing those doorways as a child, watching the elderly men going in and out, I used to wonder what went on upstairs: mah jong? opium? Probably they were playing crib, but the flavour was of Shanghai and Kowloon, warlords and ancient sages. Later, as an Air Cadet at Abbotsford airbase, I shared a room with L.A.C. Wong and A.C.l. Yee, but they were not warlords or sages; they were just Wayne and Stan, good fellows to have on your side in a waterfight.

Hardly anyone comes from Vancouver. The last place I lived in the city I had a Dane next door and a Czech in the basement. Beyond the Dane was an Englishman, down the road a brace of Russians. The Dane, Poul Hansen, had a toy shop on Robsonstrasse, so named for its bewildering variety of immigrants with bakeries, delicatessens, schnitzel houses, import shops and other ventures. Even the mayor, in the days of my childhood, was Fred Hume, who had done his apprenticeship as mayor of neighbouring New Westminster.

I'm not even a true native myself. I have a son and two brothers who were born in Vancouver. I was actually born in Toronto, sorra be on me, though I emigrated unusually early, at the age of two. Go west, young man! And don't forget your pottie.

201

Still, if I have a home town it is crass, soggy, alluring Vancouver, the only city in which I will ever be young. The home of the Polar Bear Swim, in which lunatics plunge into the freezing ocean on New Year's Day, demonstrating the alleged mildness of the climate. A city where a home sixty years old is treasured as an historic site, and properly so: before it was built, no structure had ever graced the spot. A city where the chuckles of tycoons are drowned out by the crash of timber falling up the coast, the roar of heavy machinery strip-mining the Kootenays, the crackle of gracious mansions in the West End as the bulldozers drive through them, clearing the ground for another high-rise. Soon that, too, will be history: there is hardly a house still standing.

But there is no place on earth like it: the relentless drive of the robber barons opposed by the most intransigent socialists in Canada, the damp and dreamy atmosphere of huge trees in a harbour mist, the gung-ho confidence that a downtown spiky with high-rises limned against the blue and white mountains is a vision of what a city should be—as perhaps it is, one thinks, looking north across False Creek on a rare crisp day in winter. All that rain produces the softest, sweetest water I know: what comes from the taps will foam in the tub, slip down the throat like wine crystal-cold from the mountains. Tawdry and romantic, bourgeois and raunchy at once, Vancouver is where the small ambitions flourish and the large dreams move furtively. Paradise will be Spanish Banks in the sunlight. Purgatory will be Marpole in the rain.

Who can be objective about a home town? Everything happened there for the first time. I learned to drive on Alberni Street, the choked back alley of Georgia. After that I was relaxed at Hyde Park Corner, unfazed by the Etoile. My sexual education began in the back seat of an old Plymouth parked at Wreck Beach, in the University of British Columbia endowment lands. My college education began a couple of miles further west. My political education began when Howard Green, who had apparently represented Vancouver Quadra in Parliament since old Captain Quadra himself sailed into Burrard Inlet from Spain, told me that a young lecturer at UBC was a Russian spy; and Jack Wasserman, the gossip columnist who was in business even then, suggested that the whole uproar was caused by the presence of Igor Gouzenko on campus. Was Gouzenko there, hiding from the vengeance of the Kremlin? I didn't know then. I don't know now. I wouldn't be surprised.

And UBC, where my awkward, lightweight, gutsy father broke his arm in the first quarter of the first game of the football season back in the twenties, and then, the next year, broke his collarbone. After that he became team manager instead, and the team went on after the season ended to form what eventually became Beta Theta Pi fraternity. Of which, naturally, I eventually became a member. Before that, I remember, we used to sneak into the football games at Varsity Stadium through a broken plank at the south end of the fence. It's probably still broken, and kids probably still use it, though the university is five times the size it was then.

My father claimed to have known Walter Gage as a young man. I don't believe this: I believe God imagined Walter Gage sometime around the turn of the century, and then built the university around him. Beaming benignly, walking with the gait of a king penguin unaccountably gifted as a teacher of mathematics, smoking cigarettes through a long skinny holder, Gage was, when I first met him, lumbered with some unwieldy title like Dean of Administrative and Inter-Faculty Affairs. He had an office in the Buchanan Building with a sign on the door that said DEAN GAGE, a memory like flypaper for names and faces, and a habit of throwing an arm over your shoulder as he ushered you out of the office. Whatever the title, his real function was Fixer of Student Problems. If you needed special permission for anything, were running out of money, contemplated suicide or marriage, you went to see Dean Gage.

When I last saw him he was in the same office, with the same sign. He told me some stories about my father, who had progressed from the football team to the faculty before his death in 1951, inquired about my mother and brothers, said that "Oh, yes, he was still teaching mathematics," and threw an arm over my shoulders as he ushered me out of the office.

The difference is that at the time – 1971 – he was supposed to be the President of the university. Now a story is abroad that he has retired. I don't believe that, either. UBC without Gage is like sea-water without salt: it looks the same, but the characteristic taste is gone.

For me, you see, Vancouver is indissolubly fused with the university: my family lived out that way, my father both studied and taught there, eventually I both studied and taught there myself. For thousands of Vancouverites, the university barely exists, a matter which has given some concern to W.A.C. Bennett's feisty successor, Dave Barrett. When I lived in B.C., Dave Barrett was a social worker noisily fired from the provincial prison at Haney for participating in socialist politics while engaged in the Social Credit civil service. I never met him, though our wives were briefly associated in Voice of Women. But the difference between Bennett and Barrett is the difference between stupid certainty and cautious hope.

Barrett seems to have shaken things up on all fronts, praise God, Who Alone knows how badly they needed shaking. When I return to B.C. now, I am assured on all sides that the Barrett government has made foolish mistakes, has moved too quickly, too drastically and too thoughtlessly on ideas like auto insurance and the freezing of farmland, and has then had to back off and introduce refinements which should have been included in the first place. One old friend, a beloved reactionary, grunts that this shows the hopeless incompetence and arrogance of socialists. Another, a hopeful idealist, says that it shows merely that if you've never formed a government before, you're not going to do it perfectly at once. The old pickup truck has been traded in on an Audi Fox. Can we really handle the damn thing? Is it safe? Is it practical?

I haven't lived in Vancouver since 1964, and a lot of water has passed through Lion's Gate since then. In my day, young feller, there were no hippies, there was no Gastown, no think-ins or be-ins, no town fool, no *Georgia Straight.* I missed out on the whole reign of Tom Terrific Campbell, the developer-mayor who wanted to use the authority of the War Measures Act to clean out all the hippies. My Vancouver was sedate and somnolent, and a great deal of it has been buried and bulldozed. It offered no Gran-ville Street mall, no Toronto-Dominion tower glaring down from the site of the old Hotel Vancouver. I heard Benny Goodman's big band at the Denman Auditorium. The big band has been dissolved, and the auditorium demolished. That's how old I am, sonny.

What was it like then, growing up in Vancouver in the 'forties and 'fifties? There's a rage now for the 'fifties, people looking back at the days of St. Laurent and Eisenhower with fond nostalgia. The nostalgia, believe me, is misplaced. Perhaps it always is.

What I remember about the 'fifties is boredom and panic, and the mindless boosterism of perhaps the last innocents in history. Boredom because the world seemed so thoroughly managed, so entirely under control, the career paths so utterly mapped out that we could hardly imagine the magnificence the world might offer. Suffering through the interminable dullness of Lord Byng High School, we foresaw the future: UBC, law or medicine or accounting or teaching, marriage, kids, a house on a street like the one we had grown up on, retirement, pension, death.

Panic: surely life might offer more than this, but what? We couldn't say. In 1954, a kid–Jimmy Johnston, if I recall–graduated from Lord Byng, and in the annual it said his ambition was to build his own schooner and sail it to the South Seas. I hope he did. At the time everybody took it as a spasm of wit. People like us didn't do such interesting things.

I remember a curious sense, too, that history was irrelevant, that the news was something happening elsewhere–in New York or Rome, in Sharpeville or even Ottawa–but never in Vancouver. I never read a novel set in Vancouver: I never even *heard* of one. History had taken place in England, in China, in Quebec, but not in B.C. It is no accident that I finally settled in the most ancient, storied part of Canada, where French sailors were fishing in the time of Shakespeare. A recent book, indeed, suggests that Prince Henry Sinclair, Earl of Orkney, may have sailed to Nova Scotia in 1398, a century before Columbus. Vancouver's fretfulness, its ceaseless growth, its frantic insistence on Now and Tomorrow, perhaps, shaped my taste for a community with a sense of Yesterday as well.

One takes with the left hand, relinquishes with the right. If Nova Scotia is enriched and intimidated by its memories, British

Columbia is malleable, incoherent, and splendidly free of the burdens of the past. A Nova Scotian once told me that Maritimers know from experience that nothing significant can be done about anything important, and they are wrong; whereas Westerners believe anything can be done, and done at once, and they are wrong too. In such matters Vancouver has marked me forever.

People can, dammit, build a better world; and yet in the 'fifties I could hardly see how. Long ago, in 1957, when I was nineteen, John Diefenbaker strode across the country; he was sworn in on my twentieth birthday. When an enthusiastic campus Tory introduced him in the university auditorium that spring as the new leader of the Conservative Party and "the next Prime Minister of Canada," the hall rocked with involuntary laughter. Why, the man was a *Conservative*! We had grown up in a one-party state, ruled by Liberals since before we were born.

Three years earlier, the French had been defeated at some place called Dienbienphu, and the Americans were slowly taking up the white man's evil burden in Indochina. A woman named Rosa Parks said No, she was not going to take a back seat in the buses of Montgomery, Alabama, and a young preacher named Martin Luther King got involved in something called a boycott. At Harvard University a couple of psychologists named Timothy Leary and Richard Albert were experimenting with stuff called lysergic acid, or LSD for short. In England, some Merseyside kids named Lennon and McCartney were making themselves into musicians. The seeds of the 'sixties were germinating.

For me, I suppose, it was John Diefenbaker who revealed that the world need not always be dull and over-organized, and for two or three years I was an ardent Conservative. "Follow John" is a joke now, scarcely less mouldy than "Twenty-three skidoo," but in those days John Diefenbaker meant sunlight and fresh air, and I can never look upon him with indifference. And–this is the point–Diefenbaker happened to me in Vancouver.

A home town, perhaps, is the place where the great events happened to you personally. It doesn't matter what the history books say: when I was eight years old, living on West 23rd Avenue, Japan capitulated, and we drove through the downtown streets among the screaming laughing crowds, with soldiers and drunks sitting on the fenders of our 1939 Plymouth, horns blowing, bells ringing, all the world gone crazy with joy and relief. I woke up groggy one morning, not wanting to go to school, and my mother called down the stairs that school was called off because George VI had died. Hallelujah, I muttered, and snuggled down into the blankets. John Kennedy was shot in the rain on the UBC campus, just after I had dismissed a class of freshmen.

What is all this to you, really? Why should you care whose bra straps I fumbled with, and where, or how I stole car accessories and wished to grow taller? What difference can it make that I worked as a car-hop in a drive-in called The Dog House, which specialized in hot dogs–the Mutt, the Chihuahua, the Prairie Dog. A yard-long Poodle, top of the line, would set you back three bucks. Can it matter to you that I loaded boxcars for CP Express and woke in the mornings to the melancholy *Beeee-ohhh*! of the foghorns down in the distant harbour? You never knew Rod Atkins, who was in my class in Grade Four and skipped Grade Five. He sat with me in philosophy classes ten years later all through the fall before he was killed when his Reserve Air Force plane collided with another during exercises over Squamish.

But when I think of Vancouver, those are the things I remember, the things which made me whatever I am. My Vancouver is, at last, mine alone, the place I first met sex, death, politics, learning. My Vancouver is a city fixed in time as well as place, only one of the million Vancouvers each of its people knows. You can move away from a home town, but you can never really leave it behind, because that unique city which revealed itself to you lives on in your attitudes, your ideas, your vision of the world.

It even lives on in my teeth. The next time you hear someone say Vancouver is not a Canadian city, remember my broken incisors. Vancouver has no natural ice and few artificial rinks; when we played hockey, we played on the street, on roller skates. I fell on the pavement one day, aged about twelve, and chipped a front tooth. That Saturday I went to Dr. Hallman, who told me it didn't matter much. I went from his office down to the game a block from home, and faced off with Billy Weeks. We slashed for the puck, Billy's stick glanced off mine, then flew up and smashed off half the other incisor. Within the hour I was back in Dr. Hallman's office, bleeding freely. He told me that when I got older we'd put a cap on it. I never bothered.

Vancouver an un-Canadian city? Then why was I hunched over the little mantel radio dreaming of stickhandling, listening to Foster Hewitt in Toronto screaming "He shoots—HE SCORES!"? Why did I flee California for Vancouver after a year of graduate study? How come I could tell an American from Bellingham the moment he opened his mouth, while even a kid from miserable old Toronto became one of us a week after moving in? No, no. Vancouverites know surprisingly little about Canada. One of the things they often don't know is how Canadian they are.

I come from Vancouver. What does that mean?

It means I think of mountains as friendly, and I will never be at home away from the sea. Yokohama and Vladivostok seem as near to Canada, for me, as London and Naples. I consider soft water a birth-right, and I am personally insulted by blizzards. I doubt that I would ever return to live in Vancouver; I am at home in Nova Scotia as I never was in my home town. But when Nova Scotians decamp for British Columbia, as hundreds do every year, I understand why they are going.

Coming from Vancouver means that, however sheepishly I admit it, however I might wish to deny it, something in me rejoices to hear on the roof the steady drumming of a determined, pouring rain.

(March, 1975)